Mountain Biking
Grand Junction
and Fruita

SECOND EDITION

BOB D'ANTONIO

FALCONGUIDES ®

GUILFORD, CONNECTICUT
HELENA, MONTANA
AN IMPRINT OF THE GLOBE PEQUOT PRESS

FALCONGUIDES®

Copyright © 2002 Morris Book Publishing, LLC
Previously published by Falcon Publishing, Inc. in 2000

Falcon and FalconGuides are registered trademarks of Morris Book Publishing,
LLC.

Cover photo by Bob D'Antonio
All black-and-white photos by Bob D'Antonio unless otherwise noted.
Maps by Eric West

Library of Congress Cataloging-in-Publication Data
D'Antonio, Bob.
    Mountain biking Grand Junction and Fruita / Bob D'Antonio.—
        2nd ed. p. cm.—(A Falcon guide)
    Includes index.
    ISBN 978-0-7627-1226-7
    1. All terrain cycling—Colorado—Grand Junction Region—
Guidebooks. 2. All terrain cycling—Colorado—Fruita Region—
Guidebooks. 3. Bicycle trails—Colorado—Grand Junction Region—
Guidebooks. 4. Bicycle trails—Colorado—Fruita Region—Guidebooks.
5. Grand Junction Region (Colo.)—Guidebooks. 6. Fruita Region
(Colo.)—Guidebooks. I. Title. II. Series.

GV1045.5.C62 G733 2002
796.6'3'0978817—dc21

                                                            2001054310

Manufactured in the United States of America
Second Edition/Fifth Printing

> To buy books in quantity for corporate use
> or incentives, call **(800) 962–0973**
> or e-mail **premiums@GlobePequot.com.**

Contents

About the Author

Bob D'Antonio lives in Louisville, Colorado, with his wife, Laurel, and his three children. He is a native of Philadelphia, Pennsylvania, and has spent many hours biking, climbing, and hiking throughout the United States. Bob has been mountain biking since 1982 and has written several regional mountain biking guides for Falcon Publishing. During his 27 years of climbing, Bob has established over 600 first-ascent rock climbs in the United States and has authored three rock climbing guides.

Bob's previous FalconGuides include: *Rock Climbing Colorado's San Luis Valley; Classic Rock Climbs #04 Garden of the Gods/Pikes Peak, Colorado; Classic Rock Climbs #03 Mueller State Park/Elevenmile Canyon, Colorado;* and *Mountain Biking Denver/Boulder.* He is currently working on other FalconGuide titles.

Foreword

I saw it in print but I could hardly believe it. "It's . . . Moab, Crested Butte, Marin, and Fruita," the article in *Bike* magazine read. If I had predicted five years ago that Fruita would be ranked among the top mountain biking destinations in the United States, everyone would have laughed out loud. Fruita was a pretty quiet, okay very quiet, town just west of Grand Junction, Colorado. Home to less than 4,000 people and, in that day, not even one coffee shop. Wow, how things have changed.

In 1995, while we were preparing to open Over the Edge Sports in Fruita, a small band of locals began looking for new mountain biking areas. Exploring and developing the cow trails north of Fruita began to yield more and more of the finest singletrack we had ever ridden. The first ride off 18 Road was the Vegetarian, now used in a modified version for a racecourse. But the potential of the Book Cliffs was revealed farther up where a rare stand of scrub juniper made a small forest in the high desert. The first of the newfound stuff we named Prime Cut in dishonor of the cows and because it's one of the best singletracks anywhere. Prime Cut was used to develop many of the Book Cliffs rides and is still used to start them today. First it led to Joe's Ridge (aka Joe's Cutoff), our first loop, followed soon after by Chutes and Ladders. But still the fondest memory of all—and the trophy ride—is The Edge. Scouted and explored for thousands of hours, by foot, by airplane, and by jeep, The Edge is a 30-mile loop we envisioned long before it ever looked possible. We knew we wanted a loop that took us all the way up top, and we set out to make it a reality. It was a Sunday afternoon when Tom Nix made the first official connection and we had our loop! In 1999 the International Mountain Biking Association (IMBA) honored The Edge as its first IMBA Epic Ride. We are proud of this ride, you'll be proud when you finish it, and we all owe thanks to those who spent the hours to make it a reality. The Book Cliffs area is our local favorite. Known for its narrow singletrack trails, it never ceases to impress and challenge the most skilled of mountain bikers.

The Kokopelli Trail, the pearl of the area, runs west from Fruita to Moab, Utah. The Kokopelli Trail has developed from a couple of contrived loops using gravel roads to a singletrack playground. The new Horsethief Bench Trail and Steve's Loop have made the area the most popular in the valley. It is used by hundreds of locals and thousands of visitors each year. Concerns over user impact are at an all-time high, and efforts are being made to preserve this popular destination for all to enjoy.

The Fruita Fat-Tire Festival began in 1996 and takes place the last weekend in April every year. It brings more than 1,000 of the coolest mountain bike people in the world to Fruita for a festival built around riding, having fun, and enjoying the people that make up our sport. It is an event not built around racing but rather built around the love of good singletrack (as well as an affection for good times and great beer). I am proud of the festival and love the people we meet through it. I am also deeply concerned about the impact that high numbers of mountain bikers can have. Many of the Fruita locals have made it their passion to see that the visitors to Fruita use our trails in a way that leaves them as narrow and clean as they found them.

Not enough can be said about the impact of mountain biking. The vehicles we ride and love have the potential to let us be the lowest-impact users on the trail. Only the bad habits of some users make our bikes into tools of destruction. I am frightened by the increasing number of off-trail tracks I see in Fruita and everywhere I ride. Mountain bikers must, as a group, learn to become better users if we want to be welcomed and respected on the trails we love. There is no need to make new tracks in the dirt, not ever. Sure, we all make mistakes and go off the line sometimes; mistakes happen. But willful off-trail riding to avoid an obstacle, pass another rider, miss a bump, or for any other reason is unacceptable. Off-trail riding is not welcomed in Fruita and should be cleansed from our sport. Singletrack is the essence of mountain biking. Off-trail riding is the enemy (and eventually the End!) of singletrack. Please join us in trying to make mountain biking a low-impact sport and keep our trails narrow and beautiful. Also understand that even those tracks that stray just a few inches off the trail are off-trail tracks. Our local rule of thumb: Never make a new track off the trail and you'll never be the one to ruin the singletrack. Yield to other riders by stopping in the trail and then stepping to the side; *do not* ride off to the side of the trail to pass or to yield. This bad habit is the number one cause of trail widening. We all love the outdoors and need to hold ourselves and our friends to a high standard of low-impact riding and camping. Together we can preserve and expand the world of fabulous singletrack. Thanks for reading this and thanks for joining the effort. Keep singletrack single!

So, welcome to Fruita. It's amazing how quickly the world has discovered us. We hope you come and have a wonderful time here. If you come two years in a row, you're bound to see this town change a bit. Now we have a famous bike shop in Over the Edge Sports. We have a wonderful coffee shop, great hotels, three pizza places, and a lot of really nice people. The locals are always seeking new singletrack and are often willing to invite visitors to come along for rides. It's a friendly place here in Fruita. All we ask is that when you come here, you treat the place gently and kindly. Be nice to our fragile soils and our 400-year-old juniper trees: Don't burn one in your fire, even if it's dead; leave it like you found it (dead juniper trees are pretty and a key part of the desert ecosystem). Be kind to other riders and don't be the one to make that new track in the soil (if you make a mistake, kick out your track with your foot). Since we all love Fruita's narrow trails, join us in the effort to preserve them forever. We hope you have a great ride here. Expect a little challenge to your riding skills, to your ethics, and to your tolerance for fun. I, for one, am proud of the trails here and hope you are too. Enjoy.

Special thanks to all the locals who made these trails and fight so hard to keep them narrow and clean. You all are the backbone of our sport and the hope of our future. Thanks so much to all of you and to all like you who fight for mountain biking in your area. Become an advocate in your area and in ours. Thanks.

Dedicated to all who "dig the dirt"!

Troy Rarick
Fruita Fat-Tire Festival
Over the Edge Sports
Edge Cycles Company

Acknowledgments

The Grand Junction/Fruita area is a very special place to pursue and enjoy the sport of mountain biking. The desert environment of the Colorado Plateau is one of the most visually striking areas in the world, and to pedal a mountain bike through this landscape is a privilege. So with very little fanfare and immense gratitude, I would like to thank the following people. To my sons, Adam and Jeremy, thanks for your support and the times we have spent riding together. I will always remember our adventures through this beautiful land. A special thanks to Greg Hand for the support, time, and effort he made to ride with me. To my daughter, Rachael, it's your turn to ride with me on the next project, so get ready. To Troy, Rondo, and the staff at Over the Edge Sports, a big heartfelt thank you. You guys are the best. Thanks for all the information and support on this project. Your bike shop is a great asset to the area and your commitment to the sport of mountain biking in the Grand Valley is deeply appreciated. I, for one, would like to say thanks for all your hard work. To the International Mountain Bicycling Association, Colorado Plateau Mountain Biking Association, Bureau of Land Management, and all the other public and private parties that have worked long and hard on the trails, thanks for keeping them open so people like me can come to Grand Valley and enjoy some of the best mountain biking in the world. Thanks to the folks at Falcon Publishing for all their hard work that made this project happen. To my wife, Laurel, thanks for your love and support on yet another of these projects. Without your support, none of these projects would have seen fruition.

Bob D'Antonio

MAP LEGEND

 Singletrack		(37) Trailhead
Unimproved Road		(37) Route Marker
Paved Road		X Elevation/Peak
Gravel Road		(15) Interstate
Interstate		(12) U.S. Highway
Forest/Park Boundary		(200) State Highway/County Road
Waterway		88 Forest Road
Lake/Reservoir		℗ Parking Area
Meadow/Swamp		•—• Gate
Cliff		▲ Building
Power line		++++++ Railroad
N ⬆ Scale/Compass		🛏 Picnic Area
		✈ Airport

0   1   2   3
Miles

Grand Junction and Fruita

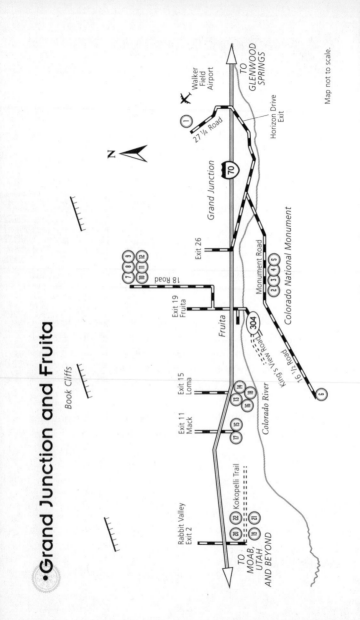

Map not to scale.

Get Ready to Crank!

Where to ride? It's a quandary that faces every mountain biker, beginner or expert, local or tourist.

If you're new to the area, where do you start? If you're a longtime local, how do you avoid the rut of riding the same old trails week after week? And how do you find new terrain that's challenging but not overwhelming? Or an easier ride for when your not-so-serious buddies come along?

Welcome to *Mountain Biking Grand Junction and Fruita*. Here are 22 rides ranging from easy doubletrack routes to smooth singletrack to bravado-busting boulder fields. The rides are described in plain language, with accurate distances and ratings for physical and technical difficulty. Each entry offers a wealth of detailed information that's easy to read and use, from an armchair or on the trail.

My aim is threefold: to help you choose a ride that's appropriate for your fitness and skill level; to make it easy to find the trailhead; and to help you complete the ride safely, without getting lost. Take care of those basics and fun is bound to break loose.

The Grand Junction/Fruita Area:
What to Expect

The rides in the Grand Junction/Fruita area cover a wide variety of terrain, from desert flats and mountains to forested mountain ridges. The trails can be steep and rough, and the weather—well, the record summer temperature in the Grand Junction/Fruita area is 110 degrees F. In the summertime there is little relief from the ever-present sun. At high elevations summer thunderstorms are common, and snow falls in the winter.

Rugged terrain requires preparedness. Get in good shape before you attempt these rides, and know your limits. Clean and maintain your bike frequently. Before each ride, check tires, rims, brakes, handlebars, seat, shifters, derailleurs, and chain to make sure they survived the last ride and are functioning properly.

A helmet is essential for safe mountain biking; it can save your life and prevent serious injuries. Cycling gloves are another essential piece of safety equipment that can save hands from cuts and bruises due to falls, encroaching branches, and rocks. They also improve your grip and comfort on the handlebars.

Always pack at least one (filled) water bottle, preferably two (or the equivalent). Rides in the Grand Junction/Fruita area are very hot in the summer, and you'll want more water than usual. A gallon is not too much on long, hot rides. A snack such as fruit or sports energy bars can keep those mighty thighs cranking for hours and prevent the dreaded "bonk"—the sudden loss of energy when your body runs out of fuel. Dress for the weather and pack a wind- and waterproof jacket just in case, especially in the winter. The Colorado west-slope summer sun packs a wallop, even at higher altitudes where the air is cooler. Don't forget sunglasses, sunscreen, and lip balm. In wet years, insects can be a problem for a short period in the spring, and you may want to carry insect repellent.

It's wise to carry a small tool kit with appropriate tools for your bike, a spare tube, and a patch kit. A tire pump is a must. You'll want to fill your tubes with leak repair goo; the desert is full of thorns and spines. Consider thicker, thorn-resistant tubes also.

This book is designed to be easily carried in a pocket or bike bag, and the maps and ride descriptions will help anyone unfamiliar with the trails. United States Geological Survey (USGS) topographic maps can provide a more detailed view of the terrain, but ride routes may not be shown. The correct topo maps are listed for each ride. Finally—I'll say it again—always wear a helmet.

The weather on the western slope of the Colorado high desert spans the range of North American extremes. On the highest rides in the Grand Junction/Fruita area, snow is common from December through March. Summer highs routinely top 90 degrees F in the lower desert country. In general, higher elevations are cooler (by as much as 6 degrees F for every 1,000 feet) and windier. If you drive to a trailhead for a ride in the higher elevations, play it safe and take a variety of clothes in the car to match the weather you're likely to encounter.

That said, we ride here year-round. Most of the trails around the Grand Junction/Fruita area are best between October and April but can also be ridden early in the morning during the hot season. The higher-elevation trails are best from April through November, though in dry years they can be ridden all winter. The best seasons to ride are spring and fall. Bear in mind that hunting seasons may occur during the good fall riding weather. Check with the Colorado Division of Wildlife for current hunting seasons. If you choose to ride where hunts are taking place, a blaze orange vest is a sensible precaution.

Afternoon thunderstorms are common during July, August, and September. These storms often appear suddenly and can be severe, with hail, high wind, and lightning. If caught in a thunderstorm, get off high ridges and take shelter in a low-lying area or in a vehicle. Do not remain under lone trees. In the higher mountains during thunderstorm season, the mornings generally dawn sweet and clear, the air refreshed by yesterday's showers. Up here it's a good idea to complete your day's riding by noon.

The rides in this book vary from 4,000 feet to more than 9,000 feet in elevation, which means you really can ride dirt all year, somewhere.

Please stay off wet, muddy trails—the soil damage and erosion one rider can cause is simply too great.

The name of the game here is singletrack. Some of the best singletrack riding in the state of Colorado can be found in the beautiful desert around the Grand Junction/Fruita area. So respect the hard work of the many volunteers and stay on the trail.

Rules of the Trail

If every mountain biker always yielded the right-of-way, stayed on the trail, avoided wet or muddy trails, never cut switchbacks, always rode in control, showed respect for other trail users, and carried out every last scrap of what was carried in (candy wrappers and bike-part debris included)—in short, if we all *did the right thing*—we wouldn't need a list of rules governing our behavior.

The fact is most mountain bikers are conscientious and are trying to do the right thing. No one becomes good at something as demanding and painful as grunting up mountainsides by cheating. Most of us don't need rules, but we do need knowledge of what exactly is the right thing to do. Here are some basic guidelines adapted from the International Mountain Bicycling Association (IMBA) Rules of the Trail. These guidelines can help prevent damage to land, water, plants, and wildlife; maintain trail acess; and avoid conflicts with other backcounty visitors and trail users.

1. Only ride on trails that are open. Don't trespass on private land, and be sure to obtain any necessary permits. If you're not sure if a trail is closed or if you need a permit, don't hesitate to ask.

2. Keep your bicycle under control. Watch the condition of the trail at all times, and follow the appropriate speed regulations and recommendations.

3. Yield to others on the trail. Make your approach well known in advance, either with a friendly greeting or a bell. When approaching a corner, junction, or blind spot, expect to encounter other trail users. When passing others, show your respect by slowing to a walking pace.

4. Don't startle animals. Animals may be easily scared by sudden approaches or loud noises. For your safety—and the safety of others in the area as well as the animals themselves—give all wildlife a wide berth. When encountering horses, defer to the horseback riders' directions.

5. Zero impact. Be aware of the impact you're making on the trail beneath you. You should not ride under conditions where you will leave evidence of your passing, such as on certain soils after rain. If a ride features optional side hikes into wilderness areas, be a zero-impact hiker, too.

Whether you're on bike or on foot, stick to existing trails, leave gates as you found them, and carry out everything you brought in.

6. Be prepared. Know the equipment you are using, the area where you'll be riding, and your cycling abilities and limitations. Avoid unnecessary breakdowns by keeping your equipment in good shape. When you head out, bring spare parts and supplies for weather changes. Be sure to wear appropriate safety gear, including a helmet, and learn how to be self-sufficient.

How to Use This Guide

Mountain Biking Grand Junction and Fruita describes 22 mountain bike rides in their entirety.

Many of the featured rides are loops, beginning and ending at the same point but coming and going on different trails. Loops are by far the most popular type of ride, and we're lucky to have so many in the area.

Be forewarned, however: The difficulty of a loop may change dramatically depending on which direction you ride around it. If you are unfamiliar with the rides in this book, try them first as described here. The directions follow the path of least resistance and most fun (which does not necessarily mean they're easy). After you've been over the terrain, you can determine whether a given loop would be fun—or even feasible—in the reverse direction. Some trails are designated as one-way, so you don't have a choice.

Portions of some rides follow maintained dirt or even paved roads. A word about desert dirt roads: Because the weather is so stable and dry much of the year, many dirt roads, though officially maintained, don't actually receive much attention. The surface may become loose because of accumulating sand and gravel, and washboard roads can be a pain.

Each ride description follows the same format:

Number: Rides are cross-referenced by number throughout this book. In many cases, parts of rides or entire routes can be linked to other rides for longer rides or variations on a standard route.

Name: For the most part, I relied on official names of trails, roads, and natural features as shown on USGS maps. In some cases deference was given to long-term local custom.

Location: Direction and approximate distance are from Fruita or Grand Junction.

Distance: The length of the ride in miles, given as a loop, one-way (if shuttled), or out and back.

Time: A conservative estimate of how long it takes to complete the ride, for example, 1 to 2 hours. The time listed is the actual riding time and does not include rest stops. Strong, skilled riders may be able to do a given ride in less than the estimated time, while other riders may take considerably longer. Also bear in mind that severe weather, changes in trail conditions, or mechanical problems may prolong a ride.

Tread: The type of road or trail: paved road, maintained dirt road, doubletrack road, and singletrack.

Aerobic level: The level of physical effort required to complete the ride: easy, moderate, or strenuous.

    Easy: Flat or gently rolling terrain, with no steeps or prolonged climbs.

    Moderate: Some hills; the climbs may be short and fairly steep, or long and gradual. There may be short hills that less fit riders will want to walk.

    Strenuous: Frequent or prolonged climbs steep enough to require riding in the lowest gear; requires a high level of aerobic fitness, power, and endurance (typically acquired through many hours of riding and proper training). Less fit riders may need to walk.

    Many rides are mostly easy and moderate but may have short strenuous sections. Other rides are mostly strenuous and should be attempted only after a complete medical checkup and implant of a second heart, preferably a *big* one. Also be aware that flailing through a highly technical section can be exhausting even on the flats. Good riding skills and a relaxed stance on the bike save energy.

    Finally, any ride can be strenuous if you ride it hard and fast. Conversely, the pain of a lung-burning climb grows easier to tolerate as your fitness level improves.

Learn to pace yourself, and remember to schedule easy rides and rest days into your calendar.

Technical difficulty: The level of bike-handling skills needed to complete the ride upright and in one piece. Technical difficulty is rated on a scale of 1 to 5, with 1 being the easiest and 5 the hardest.

Level 1: Smooth tread; road or doubletrack; no obstacles, ruts, or steeps. Requires basic bike-handling skills.

Level 2: Mostly smooth tread; wide, well-groomed singletrack or road/doubletrack with minor ruts or loose gravel or sand.

Level 3: Irregular tread with some rough sections; slickrock, single or doubletrack with obvious route choices; some steep sections; occasional obstacles may include small rocks, roots, water bars, ruts, loose gravel or sand, and sharp turns or broad, open switchbacks.

Level 4: Rough tread with few smooth places; singletrack or rough doubletrack with limited route choices; steep sections, some with obstacles; obstacles are numerous and varied, including rocks, roots, branches, ruts, sidehills, narrow tread, loose gravel or sand, and switchbacks. Most slickrock falls in this level.

Level 5: Continuously broken, rocky, root-infested, or trenched tread; singletrack or extremely rough doubletrack with few route choices; frequent, sudden, and severe changes in gradient; some slopes so steep that wheels lift off the ground; obstacles are nearly continuous and may include boulders, logs, water, large holes, deep ruts, ledges, piles of loose gravel, steep sidehills, encroaching trees, and tight switchbacks.

I've also added plus (+) and minus (-) symbols to cover gray areas between given levels of difficulty; a 4+ obstacle is harder than a 4, but easier than a 5-. A stretch of trail rated 5+ would be unridable by all but the most skilled riders.

Again, most of the rides in this book cover varied terrain, with an ever-changing degree of technical difficulty. Some trails run smooth with only occasional obstacles, and other trails are seemingly all obstacles. The path of least resistance, or *line,* is where you find it. In general, most obstacles are more challenging if you encounter them while climbing than while descending. On the other hand, in heavy surf (boulder fields, tangles of downfall, cliffs), fear plays a larger role when facing downhill.

Understand that different riders have different strengths and weaknesses. Some folks can scramble over logs and boulders without a grunt, but they crash head over heels on every switchback turn. Some fly off the steepest slopes and others freeze. Some riders climb like the wind and others just blow . . . and walk.

The key to overcoming "technical difficulties" is practice; keep trying. Follow a rider who makes it look easy, and don't hesitate to ask for constructive criticism. Try shifting your weight (good riders move a lot, front to back, side to side, and up and down) and experimenting with balance and momentum. Find a smooth patch of lawn and practice riding as slowly as possible, even balancing in a track stand. This will give you more confidence—and more time to recover or bail out—the next time the trail rears up and bites.

Hazards: A list of dangers that may be encountered on a ride, including traffic, weather, trail obstacles and conditions, risky stream crossings, obscure trails, and other perils. Remember: Conditions may change at any time. Be alert for storms, new fences, deadfall, missing trail signs, and mechanical failure. Fatigue, heat, cold, and dehydration may impair judgment. Always wear a helmet and other safety equipment. Ride in control at all times. If a section of trail seems too difficult for you, it's cool to get off and walk your bike through the bad section.

Highlights: Special features or qualities that make a ride worth doing (as if we needed an excuse!): scenery, fun singletrack, chances to see wildlife.

Land status: A list of managing agencies or landowners. Most of the rides in this book are on public land managed by one of the cities or the Bureau of Land Management (BLM). With the help of many volunteers, the BLM has done a great job of creating a wonderful mountain bike area.

Maps: A list of available maps. The USGS map of Mesa County was used for most rides. The *Colorado Atlas and Gazetteer* published by DeLorme mapping at a scale of 1:250,000 gives a good topographic overview. USGS topographic maps in the 7.5-minute series give a close-up look at terrain. Not all routes are shown on official maps.

Access: How to find the trailhead or the start of the ride. If you're lucky enough to live near one of the rides, you may be able to pedal to the start. For most riders, it'll be necessary to drive to the trailhead.

The ride: A mile-by-mile list of key points—landmarks, notable climbs and descents, wash crossings, obstacles, hazards, major turns and junctions—along the ride. All distances were measured to the nearest tenth of a mile with a carefully calibrated cyclometer. As a result, you will find a cyclometer to be very useful for following the descriptions. Terrain, riding technique, and even tire pressure can affect odometer readings, so treat all mileages as estimates. Trails were precisely mapped using the USGS 7.5-minute topographic maps as a reference. A GPS (Global Positioning System) receiver was used to supplement more traditional methods of land navigation where landmarks were obscure.

Finally, one last reminder: The real world is changing all the time. The information presented here is as accurate and up to date as possible, but there are no guarantees out in the backcountry. You alone are responsible for your safety and for the choices you make on the trail.

If you do find an error or omission in this book, or a new and noteworthy change in a ride, I'd like to hear from you. Please write to Bob D'Antonio, c/o The Globe Pequot Press, P.O. Box 480, Guilford, CT 06437.

Elevation Graphs

An elevation profile accompanies each ride description. Here the ups and downs of the route are graphed on a grid of elevation

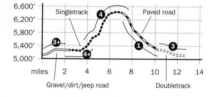

(in feet above sea level) on the left and miles pedaled across the bottom. Route surface conditions (see map legend) and technical levels are also shown on the graphs.

Note that these graphs are compressed (squeezed) to fit on the page. The actual slopes you will ride are not as steep as the lines drawn on the graphs (it just feels that way). Also, some extremely short dips and climbs are too small to show up on the graphs. All such abrupt changes in gradient are, however, mentioned in the mile-by-mile description.

The Name Game

Mountain bikers often assign their own descriptive nicknames to trails. These nicknames may help distinguish or describe certain parts of the overall ride, but only for the group of people who know the nickname. All too often the nicknames are meaningless—or misleading—to cyclists who haven't spun their pedals on the weekly group ride.

So for the sake of clarity, I stuck to the official (or at least most widely accepted) names for the trails and roads described in this book. When a route is commonly known by more than one name, the other names are mentioned. If you know them by some other name, or if you come up with nicknames that peg the personalities of these rides, then by all means share them with your riding buddies.

Roller Coaster

Location: 2 miles north of Grand Junction.

Distance: 8.2-mile loop.

Time: 1 to 1.5 hours.

Tread: 4.9 miles on singletrack; 3.3 miles on doubletrack.

Aerobic level: Moderate with very short, steep hills.

Technical difficulty: 4 on the singletrack sections; 2 on the doubletrack tread.

Hazards: There are some very steep drop-offs on the hilly sections of this ride. This is a popular area for dirt bikes and ATVs, and it can be crowded with other trail users on the weekends. It can also be confusing, with numerous trails crisscrossing each other. It is easy to get off track on this ride, but remember that it is also very easy to find your way back to the parking area. Watch out for other trail users when riding in this area.

Highlights: Wild singletrack riding on the hills near the Book Cliffs. A great area to explore the many, and I mean many, trails in this area.

Land status: BLM.

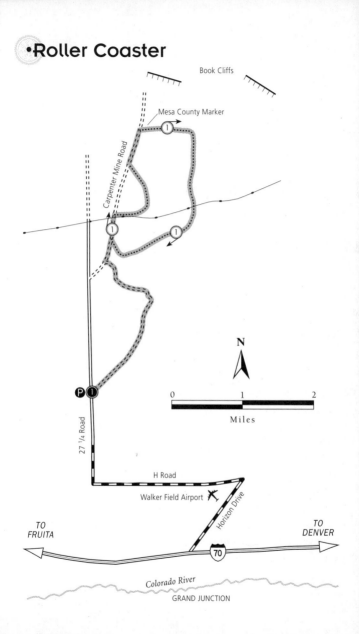

•Roller Coaster

Book Cliffs

Mesa County Marker

Carpenter Mine Road

N

0   1   2
Miles

27 ¼ Road

H Road

Walker Field Airport ✈

Horizon Drive

TO
FRUITA

TO
DENVER

70

Colorado River

GRAND JUNCTION

Maps: USGS Mesa County.

Access: Go north on the Horizon Drive exit off Interstate 70 in Grand Junction. Turn left onto H Road and go 1 mile to 27¼ Road. Go right on 27¼ Road for 1 mile to a large parking area on the right.

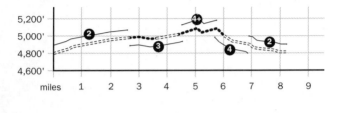

The Ride

0.0 Head north up the wide dirt road. Crank up a short hill where the dirt road ends.

0.3 Go left up a wide dirt trail.

0.4 Go right on a main trail heading toward the power lines. Angle right at all trail junctions and then head right toward 27¼ Road.

1.8 Go right on a dirt road at a BLM sign.

2.1 Pass a rusted car on the left with a dry wash on the right of the road.

2.4 A singletrack trail goes right; continue straight up the road.

2.7 Go right at the power lines to a trail junction.

2.8 Go left on a singletrack trail.

3.1 Go right.

3.2 Go left on tight singletrack up to a fence.

3.3 Go right down to the road.

3.5 Go right on the road.

3.9 Go right at a large steel Mesa County marker. Hike-a-bike across a ravine to a singletrack trail on the right.

4.0 Go right on tight singletrack heading for the hills.

4.2 Power up a series of short, steep, exposed hills. There are some very steep sections and drop-offs that you may want to walk. Use caution along this section.

4.9 Go right down steep hills toward the power lines.

5.3 Jump over a small ravine.

5.8 Follow the singletrack trail into a dry wash.

6.1 Back at the rusted car. Retrace your route to the parking area.

8.2 Arrive back at your car.

The Gunny Loop

Location: 2 miles southwest of Grand Junction.

Distance: 10.3-mile loop.

Time: 2 to 3 hours.

Tread: 0.6 mile on pavement; 3.1 miles on doubletrack; 6.6 miles on singletrack.

Aerobic level: Strenuous with a lot of steep hills.

Technical difficulty: 1 on pavement; 4 on doubletrack; 5 on singletrack.

•The Gunny Loop
•Andy's Loop
•The Ribbon

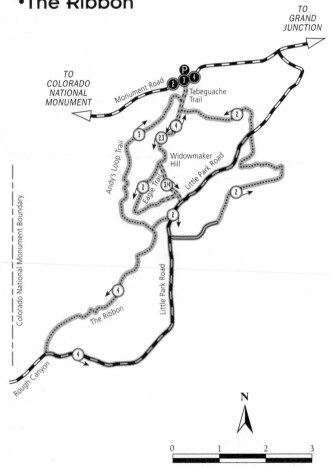

TO
GRAND
JUNCTION

TO
COLORADO
NATIONAL
MONUMENT

Monument Road

P

Tabeguache
Trail

Andy's Loop Trail

Widowmaker
Hill

Eagle Trail

Little Park Road

Colorado National Monument Boundary

Little Park Road

The Ribbon

Rough Canyon

N

0   1   2   3

Miles

Hazards: A lot of hard riding is packed into this loop. Many steep hills have drop-offs, and several technical sections run on very rocky tread. Be careful on the steep downhills back to the parking area—a fall could have dire consequences.

Highlights: One of the finest advanced rides in the Fruita/Grand Junction area. Several sections of excellent singletrack will demand your utmost attention. This ride is for the expert rider only. Mile for mile this is one of the best mountain bike rides in Colorado.

Land status: BLM.

Maps: USGS Mesa County.

Access: From Interstate 70 in Grand Junction, take exit 26. Turn left onto U.S. Highway 6 and 50 to Broadway (Colorado Highway 340). Follow Broadway over the Colorado River to Monument Road. Go left on Monument Road for 2.2 miles to a large parking area on the left. Park here to start the ride.

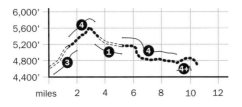

The Ride

0.0 From the parking area, go south on the wide, doubletrack Tabeguache Trail. The trail is marked with BLM trail markers.

0.4 Go right up a short, steep hill.

19

1.1 The trail forks; go right up steep, rocky tread.

1.2 A singletrack trail goes right; continue up the doubletrack trail.

1.5 Go right on the singletrack trail and pedal through an open area to the sinister-looking hill on the left.

1.6 Go right on a doubletrack that quickly turns to singletrack. Pedal through several rocky, technical sections leading up to a junction with the Eagle Trail.

2.0 Go left up a steep hill with a short portage up and over some rock.

2.3 The trail follows the ridge with some excellent views of Colorado National Monument.

2.6 Reach Eagle's Crest and the end of the climbing for now. Follow the trail down very rocky tread (4) to a junction with a doubletrack trail.

2.7 Go left down the rocky doubletrack trail to a junction with the Lunch Loop Trail.

3.5 Go right onto the Lunch Loop Trail to Little Park Road.

3.7 Go right on Little Park Road.

4.0 The Ribbon and Andy's Loop Trails go right; continue straight up the road.

4.3 Go left into the Little Park staging area. Follow the gravel road right to the well-marked Gunny Loop Trail.

5.0 Go left on the Gunny Loop Trail down to a singletrack trail on the left.

5.6 Turn left onto the tight, singletrack Gunny Loop Trail. Here's where the fun begins. Follow the awesome singletrack crossing through several gullies. You'll encounter several technical sections (4+) as you fight your way back up to Little Park Road.

8.2 Cross Little Park Road to a singletrack trail on the other side. Follow the tight singletrack to a trail junction at a house and power line.

8.5 Make a sharp left and drop down a very steep hill (4) to an open area and doubletrack trail.

8.8 Go left on the doubletrack trail, passing some cliffs on the right, to a singletrack trail on the right. Go right on the tight, singletrack trail up a short, steep hill to a trail junction.

9.3 Continue straight up a short hill.

9.6 Follow the small cairns down a very wild, steep (4) hill. Wow, what a downhill! Go right on the doubletrack road to the parking area.

10.3 Arrive back at your car.

Andy's Loop

See map on page 18.

Location: 2 miles southwest of Grand Junction.

Distance: 6.6-mile loop.

Time: 1 to 2 hours.

Tread: 3.2 miles on singletrack; 3.4 miles on doubletrack.

Aerobic level: Strenuous with some big hills.

Technical difficulty: 5 on singletrack; 4 on doubletrack.

Hazards: There are some very technical sections with dire consequences if you fall. The downhill singletrack off Little Park Road is especially dangerous. Use common sense on this section. This is a popular trail with horseback riders, runners, hikers, and cyclists, so please be courteous to all trail users.

Highlights: This is one of the best short rides in the Grand Junction area. Steep canyons, dry riverbeds, and volcanic rocks are just a few of the highlights you will encounter on this ride. The singletrack section wanders through a lunar landscape that will leave you with an unforgettable mountain bike experience.

Land status: BLM.

Maps: USGS Mesa County.

Access: From Interstate 70 in Grand Junction, take exit 26. Turn left onto U.S. Highway 6 and 50 to Broadway (Colorado Highway 340). Follow Broadway over the Colorado River to Monument Road. Go left on Monument Road for 2.2 miles to a large parking area on the left. Park here to start the ride.

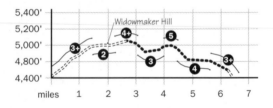

The Ride

0.0 From the parking area, go south on the wide, doubletrack Tabeguache Trail. The trail is marked with BLM trail markers.

0.4 Go right up a short, steep hill.

1.1 The trail forks; go right up steep, rocky tread.

1.2 A singletrack trail goes right; continue straight up the doubletrack trail.

1.5 Go right on the singletrack trail and pedal through an open area to the sinister-looking hill on the left.

1.6 Go left up the steep, hideous Widowmaker Hill (4). After the hill, the tread becomes loose and rocky; continue straight to a trail junction.

2.0 Go straight down a short, steep (4) rocky section to a dry wash. Pedal up to Little Park Road.

2.4 Go right on Little Park Road. Look for a singletrack trail on the right, just as the road goes up a hill.

2.7 Go right on tight singletrack. Drop your seat and get ready for a wild, rocky, dangerous (5) downhill section to a dry creekbed. Feel free to walk this section—you won't be the first.

3.2 Go right up the dry creekbed to a rock shelf. The cliffs through this section are very bizarre.

3.5 Go right up a steep hill, pushing your bike and following the rock cairns.

3.6 Top out on a ridge and continue straight on wild, tight singletrack.

3.7 Enjoy the spectacular views out to the Book Cliffs and Colorado National Monument. Follow the tight, twisting singletrack through several dry creekbeds and wild landscape to a trail junction at a large boulder.

5.5 Go right up the steep (4) hill to a trail junction at the top.

5.6 Go left on the fast, tight, sometimes rocky singletrack trail to the parking area.

6.6 Wow! What a ride. Arrive back at your car.

The Ribbon

See map on page 18.

Location: 2 miles southwest of Grand Junction.

Distance: 12.8-mile loop.

Time: 2.5 to 4 hours.

Tread: 3.6 miles on singletrack; 4.8 miles on doubletrack; 4.4 miles on paved road.

Aerobic level: Strenuous with some big hills.

Technical difficulty: 5- on singletrack; 4 on doubletrack.

Hazards: This ride has some very technical sections with dire consequences if you fall. The downhill off Little Park Road is especially dangerous due to fast speeds and car traffic. Use common sense on this section. This ride is very remote, and I recommend doing it with another person or a group of cyclists. You are *out* there on this ride. There are long climbs, big exposure, difficult route finding, and very little margin for mistakes. Be careful.

Highlights: This is one of the best advanced rides in the area. The scenery is spectacular, and the trail winds through some of the more bizarre landscape you will see here. The uphill section on the main ribbon is mind boggling. The view on top of The Ribbon is fantastic and offers panoramic views of the Book Cliffs, Colorado National Monument, and Grand Mesa.

Land status: BLM.

Maps: USGS Mesa County.

Access: From Interstate 70 in Grand Junction, take exit 26. Turn left onto U.S. Highway 6 and 50 to Broadway (Colorado Highway 340). Follow Broadway over the Colorado River to Monument Road. Go left on Monument Road for 2.2 miles to a large parking area on the left. Park here to start the ride.

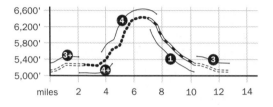

The Ride

0.0 From the parking area, go south on the wide, doubletrack Tabeguache Trail. The trail is well marked with BLM trail markers.

0.4 Go right up a short, steep hill.

1.1 The trail forks; go right up steep, rocky tread.

1.2 A singletrack trail goes right; continue up the doubletrack trail.

1.5 Go right on the singletrack trail and pedal through an open area to the sinister-looking hill on the left.

1.6 Go left up the steep, hideous Widowmaker Hill (4). After the hill, the tread becomes loose and rocky; continue straight to a trail junction.

2.0 Go straight down a short, steep (4) rocky section to a dry wash. Pedal up to Little Park Road.

2.4 Go right on Little Park Road. Look for a singletrack trail on the right, just as the road goes up a hill.

2.7 Go right on tight singletrack. Drop your seat and get ready for a wild, rocky, dangerous (5) downhill section to a dry creekbed. Feel free to walk this section—you won't be the first.

3.2 Go left up the dry creekbed to a rock shelf. The cliffs through this section are very bizarre.

3.5 Singletrack trail goes right; continue straight to a rock shelf.

3.6 Go up the short, rocky (4) technical section to level ground. Follow the singletrack with big exposure on your right.

3.9 Drop down on tight tread into a ravine. Push your bike through a short section to a slickrock ribbon on the right.

4.0 Go up the small, tight ribbon on great singletrack. Look left down to the bizarre water grooves in the dry creekbed.

4.3 Go left over the ridge and up a larger ribbon to a trail on the left.

4.4 Go left over a small ridge, then drop down on soft, sandy tread to the main ribbon. Go right up the incredible, steep expanse of slickrock. Stay left near the water groove.

5.0 Take a rest here and enjoy the views. The climbing is not over yet. Follow the singletrack through a sandy area up another section of steep riding.

5.3 Top out and follow the singletrack through weird, Jabba the Hutt–looking mounds of rock. Hike your bike up a steep section to the final climb.

5.4 Go up the large slickrock slab to the end of The Ribon.

5.8 Drop down off The Ribbon and follow the wide doubletrack road to Little Park Road.

6.0 Go left down Little Park Road. Watch out for car traffic and keep your speed in check.

10.4 Go left and retrace your route to the parking area.

12.8 Arrive back at your car. Bust open a few cold beers—you deserve 'em!

Mira Monte/Lower Gunny Loop

Location: 2 miles southwest of Grand Junction.

Distance: 9.1-mile loop.

Time: 2 to 2.5 hours.

Tread: 5 miles on singletrack; 3 miles on paved road; 1.1 miles on doubletrack.

Aerobic level: Moderate with some short, steep climbs.

Technical difficulty: 4 on singletrack; 5 on Widowmaker Hill.

Hazards: There are a number of technical sections and steep drop-offs on this great loop. Be careful, especially on your first time through.

Highlights: This is a great ride that favors the singletrack lover. There are steep climbs, rocky, technical sections, and a steep—and I mean steep—hill (Widowmaker Hill) that will test the skills of any cyclist.

Land status: BLM and private.

Maps: USGS Mesa County.

Access: From Interstate 70 in Grand Junction, take exit 26. Turn left onto U.S. Highway 6 and 50 to Broadway (Colorado Highway 340). Follow Broadway over the Colorado River to Monument Road. Go left on Monument Road for 2.2 miles to a large parking area on the left. The ride starts here.

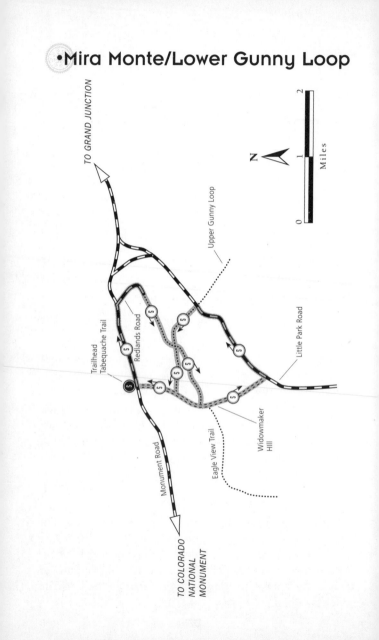

•Mira Monte/Lower Gunny Loop

TO GRAND JUNCTION

Upper Gunny Loop

N

Miles

0   1   2

Redlands Road

Little Park Road

Trailhead
Tabequache Trail

Widowmaker
Hill

Eagle View Trail

Monument Road

TO COLORADO
NATIONAL
MONUMENT

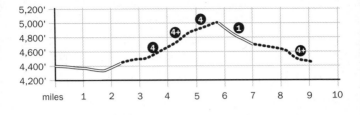

The Ride

0.0 From the parking area, pedal back down Monument Road to Redlands Road.

1.7 Go right on Redlands Road to Mira Monte Road. Continue straight on Mira Monte Road to a parking area and the start of the singletrack riding.

2.3 Turn left into the parking area and follow the singletrack trail into a dry gulch with rock cliffs on the right. Enjoy beautiful riding.

3.2 Cool, tight riding through several large sandstone boulders.

3.4 Arrive at a trail junction. Go right up a short hill with great views.

3.6 Go left at a Y junction up a steep hill (3) past several slickrock sections. This is good stuff here!

3.9 Go right onto a tight singletrack along the edge of a sandstone cliff with steep drop-offs to the right. Carry your bike through the lemon-squeeze boulder and ride up to a trail junction.

4.5 Go left up to a trail junction. Here is where things turn ugly. Pedal, push, or crawl up the steep Widowmaker Hill. Follow the doubletrack with some technical rock (4) ledges.

5.4 Eagle View Trail is on the right. Continue straight to Little Park Road.

5.6 Go left down Little Park Road. This is a fast, paved road. Watch out for car traffic.

7.0 Go left on the lower Gunny Loop Trail. Follow tight singletrack to a trail junction at a house and power line.

7.3 Make a sharp left and drop down a very steep hill (4) to an open area and doubletrack trail.

7.6 Go left on the doubletrack up to a singletrack trail on the right. Go right onto tight singletrack up a short, steep hill to a trail junction.

8.1 Continue up a short, steep hill.

8.4 Follow the rock cairns down a very wild, steep (4) hill. That was steep! Go right on the doubletrack toward the parking area.

9.1 Arrive back at your car.

Turkey Flats Loop

Location: 20 miles southwest of Grand Junction.

Distance: 9.6-mile loop.

Time: 1.5 to 2 hours.

Tread: 6.6 miles on singletrack; 3 miles on doubletrack.

Aerobic level: Moderate with a few steep climbs.

Technical difficulty: 4 on singletrack; 2 on doubletrack.

Hazards: Hunters during the season, other cyclists, and tight switchbacks with loose tread.

Highlights: A great ride to escape the heat lower down in the valley; beautiful summer flowers and great colors during the fall; excellent singletrack that wanders through a large aspen forest.

Land status: Grand Mesa National Forest.

Maps: USGS Mesa County.

Access: Follow the directions for the rides at the Tabeguache Trailhead (Rides 2, 3, and 4). Instead of parking at the trailhead parking, continue straight up Monument Road to the entrance of Colorado National Monument. Continue straight up the road to the Glade Park post office. Admission to the park is free if you tell the attendant you are going to Glade Park. At the post office turn left onto 16 Road and travel 11.9 miles, passing the Mud Springs Campground. Avoid all left turns and park at a pullout near a post marked TURKEY FLATS TRAIL. The ride starts here.

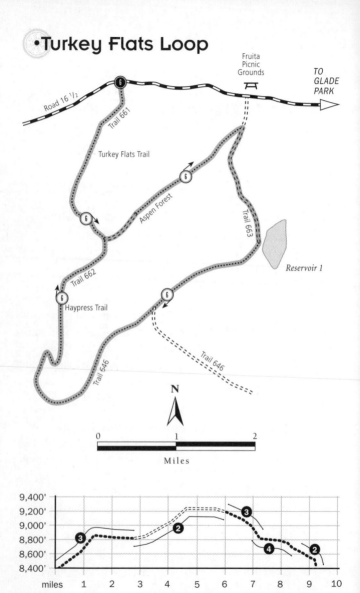

•Turkey Flats Loop

Fruita
Picnic
Grounds

*TO
GLADE
PARK*

Road 16 ½

Trail 661

Turkey Flats Trail

6

6

6

Aspen Forest

Trail 663

Reservoir 1

Trail 662

6

6

Haypress Trail

Trail 546

Trail 646

N

0   1   2

Miles

9,400'
9,200'
9,000'
8,800'
8,600'
8,400'

3

2

3

4

2

miles   1   2   3   4   5   6   7   8   9   10

The Ride

0.0 From the parking area, follow Trail 661 on excellent singletrack past a picnic table into an aspen forest.

1.5 Come to a junction with Trail 662. Continue straight on Trail 661 through a beautiful aspen grove.

2.4 Ride or push your bike through a short, steep section. The tread becomes level, then drops down to a doubletrack road.

2.8 Crank right when you reach a junction with Trail 663. Ignore all side roads.

3.3 Follow Trail 663 through a gate, then pedal along the reservoir on excellent singletrack.

3.9 The trail becomes very steep. No shame in pushing your bike here.

4.8 Come to a junction with Trail 646. Go right up a mellow hill and look for a singletrack trail on the right.

6.1 Go right onto Trail 662. Follow great singletrack down past some steep switchbacks (use caution here), then through some often wet sections to Trail 661.

8.1 Go left on Trail 661, descending excellent singletrack back to the parking area.

9.6 Arrive back at your car and some cold brews.

Prime Cut/Joe's Cutoff

Location: 8 miles north of Fruita.

Distance: 5.4-mile loop.

Time: 1 to 1.5 hours.

Tread: 0.4 mile on doubletrack; 5 miles on singletrack.

Aerobic level: Moderate.

Technical difficulty: 3+ on singletrack; 1 on doubletrack.

Hazards: You'll find some steep drop-offs on the downhill return to the parking area. This is a very popular trail with cyclists; be courteous to other trail users.

Highlights: Great singletrack riding through a high desert environment and an excellent introduction to the Book Cliffs area. The Prime Cut singletrack is one of the finest in the area. The downhill back to the parking area is sure to leave a smile on your face. Prime Cut is also the starting point for three other rides in the area.

Land status: BLM.

Maps: USGS Mesa County.

Access: From downtown Fruita, travel east on Aspen Avenue for 2 blocks to Maple Avenue (17 Road). Go left (north) on Maple Avenue for 4.1 miles to 3/10 Road. Go right on 3/10

•Prime Cut/Joe's Cutoff
•Chutes and Ladders
•Zippety Doo Daa

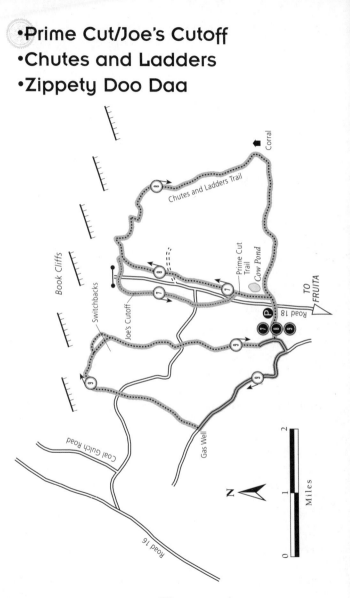

Road for 0.5 mile to 18 Road. Go left on 18 Road for 7.6 miles to a large parking area on the left. Park here to begin the ride.

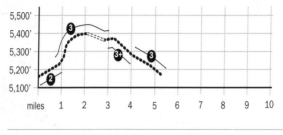

The Ride

0.0 From the parking area, cross the road to a single-track trail. Drop down the steep hill to a cow pond.

0.2 Go left at the pond to the Prime Cut singletrack trail.

0.4 The trail forks; go right, following the awesome singletrack trail that weaves through the juniper trees.

1.3 Go right on a road for a short distance to a single-track trail on the left. Go left on excellent single-track riding that leads up to a junction with the Chutes and Ladders Trail.

2.1 Go left up to a dirt road.

2.5 Go right on the road.

2.7 Cross the road and pass a gate, then follow the road down to a singletrack trail on the right.

2.8 Go right on a tight, singletrack trail through a short technical section up to a trail junction.

3.0 The Frontside Trail goes straight; go left on the Joe's Cutoff Trail.

3.6 Zip down the incredible, tight singletrack trail on a ridgeline with steep drop-offs on both sides of the trail.

3.9 The trail turns to doubletrack and dumps you on a road.

4.3 Go left on the road to a singletrack trail on the right.

4.4 Go right on a singletrack trail.

4.8 Cross over a road.

5.0 Drop down a short hill to the cow pond and go right up to the parking area.

5.4 You are back at your car.

Chutes and Ladders

See map on page 35.

Location: 8 miles north of Fruita.

Distance: 7.1-mile loop.

Time: 1.5 to 2 hours.

Tread: 6.9 miles on singletrack; 0.2 mile on doubletrack.

Aerobic level: Moderate with a few steep, short hills.

Technical difficulty: 4 on singletrack; 1 on doubletrack.

Hazards: Steep descents on tight singletrack and some drop-offs that could ruin your day.

Highlights: Great singletrack riding; one of the better rides in the Book Cliffs area. The fun factor on this ride is very high. The trail traverses along the lower part of the Book Cliffs and follows a wandering line in and out of several dry washes. Do this ride.

Land status: BLM.

Maps: USGS Mesa County.

Access: From downtown Fruita, travel east on Aspen Avenue for 2 blocks to Maple Avenue (17 Road). Go left (north) on Maple Avenue for 4.1 miles to 3/10 Road. Go right on 3/10 Road for 0.5 mile to 18 Road. Go left on 18 Road for 7.6 miles to a large parking area on the left. Park here to begin the ride.

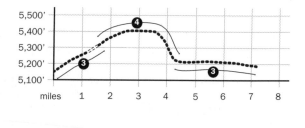

The Ride

0.0 From the parking area, cross the road to a single-track trail. Drop down the steep hill to the cow pond.

0.2 Go left at the pond to the Prime Cut singletrack trail.

0.4 The trail forks; go right, following the awesome singletrack trail that weaves through the juniper trees.

1.3 Turn right onto the doubletrack road and take an immediate left onto a singletrack trail. Go left on excellent singletrack tread that leads up to a junction with the Chutes and Ladders Trail.

2.1 Turn right onto the Chutes and Ladders Trail up a series of short, steep hills. No shame pushing your bike through this section.

2.3 Reach the top of the hill; drop down tight singletrack (3+) into a dry wash.

2.6 Drop down another steep hill.

3.0 Climb up a steep hill on tight tread; follow awesome singletrack down to a trail junction.

3.6 Go left on tight tread.

4.1 Go left and enjoy a wonderful run on tight single-track that slices through open range.

5.1 Go left down to a corral.

5.2 Go right along the fence on tight singletrack.

5.5 Cross over a dirt road.

5.8 Cross over a dirt road to singletrack trail.

6.3 Climb up a short, steep hill. Drop down a steep (3) pitch following tight singletrack through two dry washes, then make a quick run up to the cow pond.

6.9 Go left at the cow pond and climb back up to the parking area.

7.1 Arrive back at your car.

Zippety Doo Daa
See map on page 35.

Location: 8 miles north of Fruita.

Distance: 8.6-mile loop.

Time: 1.5 to 2.5 hours.

Tread: 6.3 miles on singletrack; 2.3 miles on dirt road.

Aerobic level: Strenuous with many steep hills.

Technical difficulty: 4 on singletrack; 2 on doubletrack.

Hazards: There are some serious drop-offs and steep downhills on this ride—stay off it if you walk steep downhills. If you are not comfortable on steep hills, you are only going to hurt yourself and damage the trail. Stay on the singletrack *and do not do this ride in reverse.*

Highlights: Steep downhills, excellent singletrack, and some very technical sections add up to make this one of the best expert rides in the area. The downhill sections will test the skills of most cyclists.

Land status: BLM.

Maps: USGS Mesa County.

Access: From downtown Fruita, travel east on Aspen Avenue for 2 blocks to Maple Avenue (17 Road). Go left (north) on Maple Avenue for 4.1 miles to 3/10 Road. Go right on 3/10 Road for 0.5 mile to 18 Road. Go left on 18 Road for 7.6 miles to a large parking area on the left. Park here to begin the ride.

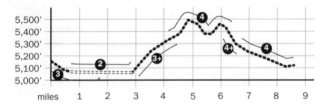

The Ride

0.0 From the parking area, go west on a singletrack trail leading out to open range.

0.3 Hop over a small fence and crank up a steep (3) hill to a trail junction.

0.7 Turn left onto a faint doubletrack trail going down to a dirt road.

1.3 Go right on the dirt road for 1.6 miles to singletrack trail on the right at a gas well.

2.9 Go right at the gas well, up a tight singletrack trail. Traverse a hill into open range.

3.4 Climb over a fence and continue straight on singletrack.

3.9 Cross over a faint doubletrack road.

4.3 Cross over a dirt road and climb up singletrack to a trail junction.

4.7 The Frontside Trail goes straight; here is where the fun begins. Go right down a short hill and drop into a technical (4) dry wash. Power through the wash and climb up steep (4+) switchbacks to the top of a hill. Go right and down an exposed ridgeline to a trail junction.

5.7 Begin a series of steep (4+) hills, the last one dropping you on a dirt road.

6.7 Go left on the road to the singletrack trail going right up the side of a hill. Go right on the singletrack trail and again climb and descend some serious (4+) hills down to a trail junction.

7.9 Go left at a familiar trail junction and retrace your route to the parking area.

8.6 Stagger back to your car.

10

Vegetarian Loop

Location: 8 miles north of Fruita.

Distance: 5.5-mile loop.

Time: 45 minutes to 1 hour.

Tread: 1.8 miles on singletrack; 3.7 miles on doubletrack.

Aerobic level: Easy with a couple of short, moderate hills.

Technical difficulty: 2 to 3 on the singletrack sections; 2 on the doubletrack.

Hazards: Some tight singletrack that some beginners might find difficult to negotiate. Watch out for other trail users on this popular trail and mountain bike area. Stay on the singletrack.

Highlights: Great introduction to the 18 Road area. Some excellent singletrack riding through a high desert environment. Access to several rides in the 18 Road area.

Land status: BLM.

Maps: USGS Mesa County.

Access: From downtown Fruita, travel east on Aspen Avenue for 2 blocks to Maple Avenue (17 Road). Go left (north) on Maple Avenue for 4.1 miles to 3/10 Road. Go right on 3/10 Road for 0.5 mile to 18 Road. Go left on 18 Road for 7.6 miles to a large parking area on the left. Park here to begin the ride.

•Vegetarian Loop

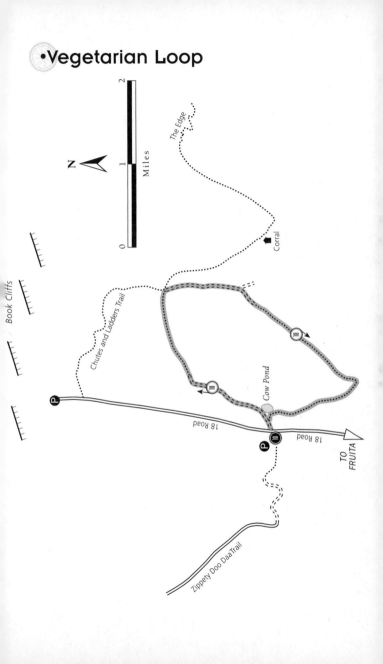

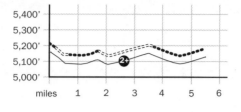

The Ride

0.0 From the parking area, cross the road to a single-track trail. Drop down the steep hill to the cow pond.

0.2 Go left at the cow pond. Follow doubletrack tread toward the Book Cliffs to a trail junction.

0.7 Continue straight on a singletrack trail. Follow the tight singletrack trail northeast to a trail junction with a doubletrack road.

1.7 Go right onto a doubletrack road.

2.5 Look for a hidden, faint doubletrack trail on the right. Turn right following the faint doubletrack. Continue straight, crossing over the singletrack Chutes and Ladders Trail. Follow the doubletrack trail down to a trail junction.

3.9 Go right on the doubletrack trail, which quickly turns to singletrack. Follow the singletrack north back to the cow pond.

5.3 Go left at the pond up a short hill, crossing 18 Road to the parking area.

5.5 Arrive back at your car.

The Frontside

Location: 8 miles north of Fruita.

Distance: 21.4 miles out and back.

Time: 2.5 to 4 hours.

Tread: 16.4 miles on singletrack; 5 miles on doubletrack.

Aerobic level: Strenuous with many hills and technical sections.

Technical difficulty: 4+ on singletrack; 3+ on doubletrack.

Hazards: Rocky sections and extreme, steep hills with drop-offs that can and will inflict damage to you and your bike if you fall. The downhill section at the turnaround point is fast, and there are many sharp turns that will demand your attention. I recommend doing this ride with another person in case any mishaps take place.

Highlights: A great ride for strong intermediate or expert riders. This ride has a lot of variety on it. Keep in mind that what goes up, must come down. Save some energy for the hills on the way back to the trailhead.

Land status: BLM.

Maps: USGS Mesa County.

Access: From downtown Fruita, travel east on Aspen Avenue for 2 blocks to Maple Avenue (17 Road). Go left (north) on Maple Avenue for 4.1 miles to 3/10 Road. Go right on 3/10 Road for 0.5 mile to 18 Road. Go left on 18 Road for 7.6 miles to a large parking area on the left. Park here to begin the ride.

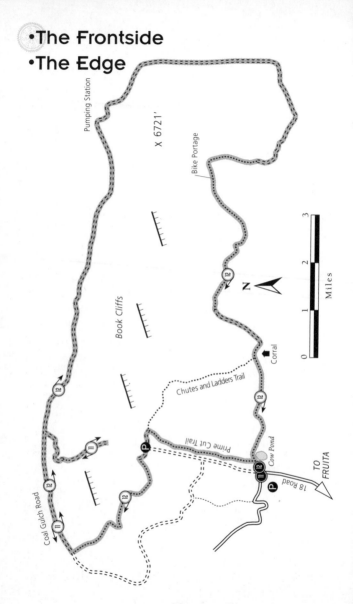

•The Frontside
•The Edge

Pumping Station

X 6721'

Bike Portage

Book Cliffs

Chutes and Ladders Trail

Corral

Prime Cut Trail

Cow Pond

Coal Gulch Road

18 Road

TO FRUITA

N

Miles

0   1   2   3

P

P

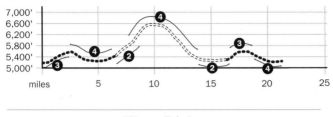

The Ride

0.0 From the parking area, cross the road to a single-track trail. Drop down the steep hill to a cow pond.

0.2 Go left at the pond to the Prime Cut singletrack trail.

0.4 The trail forks; go right, following the awesome singletrack trail that weaves through the juniper trees.

1.3 Go right on the road for a short distance to a singletrack trail on the left. Go left on excellent singletrack riding that leads up to a junction with the Chutes and Ladders Trail.

2.1 Go left up to a dirt road.

2.5 Go right on the road.

2.7 Cross the road and pass a gate, then follow the road down to a singletrack trail on the right.

2.8 Go right on a tight singletrack trail through a short technical section up to a trail junction.

3.0 Joe's Cutoff Trail goes left; continue straight on the Frontside Trail.

3.5 Cross over an exposed ridge. Steady as you go.

4.1 Come to a trail junction; continue straight.

4.2 Drop down a steep hill with tight switchbacks into a technical dry wash. Continue on obvious singletrack.

5.0 Climb up a short, steep hill to a trail junction.

5.1 Zippety Doo Daa Trail goes left; continue right on the Frontside Trail.

5.3	Drop down a short, steep hill.
5.8	Climb up a short, steep hill and make a nice run on tight singletrack out to Coal Gulch Road.
6.5	Go right on Coal Gulch Road, passing a cattle guard and an old mine to a trail on the right.
8.4	Go right up the steep, rocky doubletrack trail.
8.9	The grade eases for the moment, but don't be fooled—there is still a lot of climbing ahead.
9.7	Just when you thought it couldn't get any steeper, it does.
10.0	Enjoy the spectacular views out Grand Mesa, the Book Cliffs, and into Utah. Don't panic; you are almost at the top.
10.6	One more little hill and you are . . .
10.7	At the top. What a climb! Now you get to turn around and ride down that monster of a hill. Save some energy for hills on the way back to the car. Retrace your route to the parking area.
21.4	Arrive back at your car.

The Edge

See map on page 46.

Location: 8 miles north of Fruita.

Distance: 30-mile loop.

Time: 3 to 5 hours.

Tread: 16.6 miles on singletrack; 13.4 miles on doubletrack.

Aerobic level: Strenuous with many hills and technical sections.

Technical difficulty: 4+ on singletrack; 3+ on doubletrack.

Hazards: Rocky sections and extreme, steep hills with drop-offs that can and will inflict damage to you and your bike if you fall. This is an extremely difficult ride that should only be attempted by strong, expert cyclists. Route finding can be a problem. Carry a lot of water and some energy food, and use your common sense. Stop at Over the Edge Sports in Fruita for more information on this ride.

Highlights: A great ride for strong, expert riders. The singletrack sections are just wonderful, the downhills are fast, and the drop-offs will keep you on your toes. Expect a good workout on this ride. Go for it!

Land status: BLM.

Maps: USGS Mesa County.

Access: From downtown Fruita, travel east on Aspen Avenue for 2 blocks to Maple Avenue (17 Road). Go left (north) on Maple Avenue for 4.1 miles to 3/10 Road. Go right on 3/10 Road for 0.5 mile to 18 Road. Go left on 18 Road for 7.6 miles to a large parking area on the left. Park here to begin the ride.

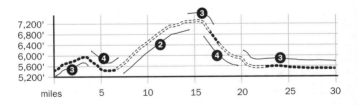

The Ride

0.0 From the parking area, cross the road to a single-track trail. Drop down the steep hill to a cow pond.

0.2 Go left at the pond to the Prime Cut singletrack trail.

0.4 The trail forks; go right, following the awesome singletrack trail that weaves through the juniper trees.

1.3 Go right on the road for a short distance to a singletrack trail on the left. Go left on excellent singletrack riding that leads up to a junction with the Chutes and Ladders Trail.

2.1 Go left up to a dirt road.

2.5 Go right on the road.

2.7 Cross the road and pass a gate, then follow the road down to a singletrack trail on the right.

2.8 Go right on a tight singletrack trail through a short technical section up to a trail junction.

3.0 Joe's Cutoff Trail goes left; continue straight on the Frontside Trail.

3.5 Cross over an exposed ridge. Steady as you go.

4.1 Come to a trail junction; continue straight.

4.2 Drop down a steep hill with tight switchbacks into a technical dry wash. Continue straight on the obvious singletrack trail.

5.0 Climb up a short, steep hill to a trail junction.

5.1 Zippety Doo Daa Trail goes left. Go right on the Frontside Trail.

5.3 Drop down a short, steep hill.

5.8 Climb up a short, steep hill and make a nice run on tight singletrack out to Coal Gulch Road.

6.5 Go right on Coal Gulch Road. Pass over a cattle guard. Continue straight up the road. Pass an old mine on the right.

8.4 The Frontside Trail goes right. Continue climbing straight up Coal Gulch Road.

12.9 Go right, climbing close to the ridgeline. Great views here. You will climb some short hills through this section. Continue following the main trail and ignore all roads to the left. Continue straight up to a pumping station.

16.8 At the pumping station go left on good tread.

17.5 Bear left here. If you pass an old green oil tank, turn around, because you have passed the turnoff.

18.4 Go right down the doubletrack trail.

19.1 Overlook to the left. Take a break and get ready for wild riding. Continue down the rutted, rocky doubletrack to a singletrack trail on the right.

20.5 Go right on the faint singletrack trail. After a little more than a mile, look for a cairn on the left.

21.7 At the cairn on the left, take the trail that leads to the streambed. This section will demand your attention.

22.4 Complete a short hike-a-bike section going right across a ravine and out of the canyon. Descend back into the streambed and follow it through a very rocky section.

22.7 Come to a BLM marker and a cairn. Go west out of the dry wash over a short hill to another dry wash. Go 0.1 mile to a marked singletrack going uphill.

24.1 Follow the awesome singletrack up and then down to a road.

25.8 Go left on the road. You are back to calmer waters.

27.0 Go right at a cairn onto singletrack. Bop down to a corral and a singletrack trail on the left.

28.0 Go left on singletrack. Follow the singletrack through several washes and up and down a steep hill to a cow pond.

29.8 Go left at the cow pond up to 18 Road and the parking area.

30.0 Arrive at your car. You survived The Edge. Take a well-deserved rest.

Loma Area

Mary's Loop

Location: 6 miles west of Fruita.

Distance: 8.5-mile loop.

Time: 1 to 2 hours.

Tread: 1.3 miles on singletrack; 4.3 miles on doubletrack; 2.9 miles on gravel.

Aerobic level: Moderate with a few short hills.

Technical difficulty: 3, with a short section of technical riding.

Hazards: Steep drop-offs just past the BLM kiosk—use extreme caution on this section and walk your bike if you are afraid of heights. Accidents can happen and have happened on this ride. Again, use caution and walk your bike if you don't feel comfortable with heights.

Highlights: Spectacular views of the Colorado River and an excellent singletrack section make this one of the best moderate rides in the area. This is a great introductory ride that should not be missed.

Land status: BLM.

Maps: USGS Mesa County.

•Mary's Loop
•Horsethief Bench

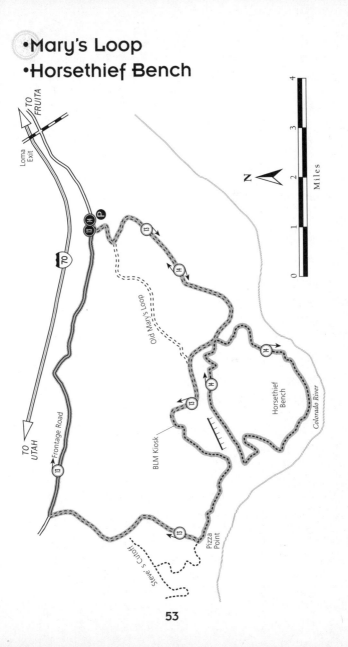

Access: From Fruita, drive 5 miles west on Interstate 70 to the Loma exit. Turn left and travel over the interstate, then turn right onto the frontage road and go 0.1 mile to the dirt road on the left. Turn left over a cattle guard and follow the road for 1.2 miles to a large parking area on the right with a BLM kiosk, day pavillion, and picnic tables.

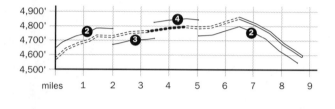

The Ride

0.0 From the parking area, go right on the dirt road, then make a quick left up the short hill following the well-marked Mary's Loop.

0.6 Go right up the rocky doubletrack trail. Cruise on excellent tread with beautiful views out to the Colorado River on the left.

1.9 Overlook to the Colorado River on the left.

2.1 The Horsethief Bench Trail goes left; continue straight to the BLM kiosk and the start of the singletrack riding.

3.3 Continue straight on tight singletrack; use caution as the trail hugs the edge of a large cliff with steep drop-offs.

3.7 Pass through a gate and crank up a short, steep hill. The tread becomes tight, rocky, and (3+) technical.

4.6 The trail turns to doubletrack; go right up to the trail junction. Lion's Loop goes left; continue up doubletrack to the top of a short hill.

6.1 Go left down the wide, fast dirt road.

6.2 Go right on the wide dirt road to the parking area.

8.5 Arrive back at your car.

Horsethief Bench

See map on page 53.

Location: 6 miles west of Fruita.

Distance: 8.5-mile loop.

Time: 1 to 2 hours.

Tread: 4.1 miles on singletrack; 4.4 miles on doubletrack.

Aerobic level: Moderate with a few short hills.

Technical difficulty: 3, with a short section of technical riding.

Hazards: Use caution on the doubletrack leading down to Horsethief Bench. There are short, rocky technical sections that can be easily walked. Watch out for steep drop-offs.

Highlights: This ride offers spectacular views of the Colorado River along with an excellent singletrack section that is one of the best in the area for those seeking a moderate ride. The singletrack section along Horsethief Bench is just pure fun. Throw in the great views out to the beautiful Colorado River and you have a wonderful mountain biking experience.

Land status: BLM.

Maps: USGS Mesa County.

Access: From Fruita, drive 5 miles west on Interstate 70 to the Loma exit. Turn left and travel over the interstate, then turn right onto the frontage road and go 0.1 mile to the dirt road on the left. Turn left over a cattle guard and follow the road for 1.2 miles to a large parking area on the right with a BLM kiosk, day pavillion, and picnic tables.

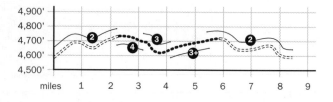

The Ride

0.0 From the parking area, go right on the dirt road, then make a quick left up the short hill following the well-marked Mary's Loop.

0.6 Go right up the rocky doubletrack trail. Cruise on excellent tread with beautiful views out to the Colorado River on the left.

1.9 Overlook to the Colorado River on the left.

2.1 Mary's Loop continues straight; you go left past the fence and drop down (4+) steep tread to the start of Horsethief Bench Loop.

2.2 Go left on awesome, tight singletrack that winds along the base of a cliff.

2.4 Great views of the Colorado River.

2.9 The trail drops down a short, steep wash, then parallels the Colorado River with steep drop-offs to the left.

3.8 The trail goes right, away from the river. A short hike-a-bike section leads to great singletrack riding.

4.9 The trail follows a dry streambed and then curves around the base of a sandstone wall on tight single-track to complete the loop.

6.0 Crank left up the short, steep hill back to the Mary's Loop Trail.

6.1 Go right on Mary's Loop, retracing your route to the parking area.

8.3 Arrive back at your car.

15

Lion's Loop

Location: 8 miles west of Fruita.

Distance: 7.1-mile loop.

Time: 1 to 2 hours.

Tread: 2.2 miles on singletrack; 3.5 miles on doubletrack; 1.4 miles on gravel.

Aerobic level: Moderate with a few steep hills.

Technical difficulty: 3+ on singletrack; a short hike-a-bike section; 3 on doubletrack.

Hazards: Rocky sections and steep drop-offs. This is a popular trail that sees a lot of traffic from cyclists, runners, and hikers. Use caution, as there are some very steep drop-offs on the singletrack sections.

•Lion's Loop
•Lower Lion's loop (Steve's Cutoff)
•Troy Built Trail

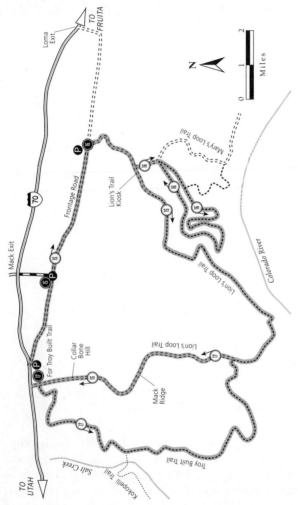

Highlights: Another great ride with excellent singletrack, some great uphills, and spectacular overlooks to the Colorado River. This is one of the must-do rides in the area. You can do this ride and easily hook up with other trails in the area for a longer and more difficult ride.

Land status: BLM.

Maps: USGS Mesa County.

Access: From Fruita, drive 5 miles west on Interstate 70 to the Loma exit. Turn left and travel over the interstate, then turn right onto the frontage road and go 0.1 mile to the dirt road on the left. Turn left over a cattle guard and follow the road for 2.9 miles to a parking area on the left at the base of a hill.

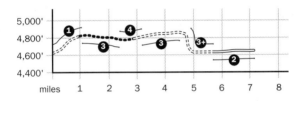

The Ride

0.0 From the parking area, go left up the short, steep dirt road.

0.2 At the top of the hill, cross over a cattle guard and drop down a doubletrack road to a trail junction.

0.7 Go right on the well-marked Lion's Loop Trail. Climb up past a register on rocky tread to level ground. This begins a great section of singletrack with great views out to the Colorado River.

1.3 The tread becomes rocky (3+), and the view out to the Colorado River becomes even more impressive.

2.6	The trail takes a sharp right up through a very rocky section. Climb off your bike and carry it through this section. The trail stays very rocky and wanders down to a junction with a dirt road.
3.0	Go right up the rocky, loose road, climbing up to a junction with Troy Built Trail.
3.8	Junction with the Troy Built Trail; continue straight on the wide, rocky dirt road.
4.8	Stay right and begin a fast downhill to the frontage road.
5.0	Bear right.
5.4	Very steep, rocky downhill.
5.7	Go right on the frontage road up to the parking area.
7.1	Arrive back at your car.

Lower Lion's Loop (Steve's Cutoff)

See map on page 58.

Location: 6 miles west of Fruita.

Distance: 8.6-mile loop.

Time: 1 to 2 hours.

Tread: 3.2 miles on singletrack; 5.4 miles on doubletrack.

Aerobic level: Moderate with a couple of short hills.

Technical difficulty: 4 on singletrack; 2 on doubletrack.

Hazards: There are some steep drop-offs on the lower loop; please use extreme caution on this section. The lower loop has short sections of rocky, technical riding on tight singletrack where most riders will have to carry their bikes.

Highlights: Incredible singletrack riding with exceptional views of the Colorado River. The singletrack on the lower loop adds to the experience. You can easily hook up with other rides to make a great outing.

Land status: BLM.

Maps: USGS Mesa County.

Access: From Fruita, drive 5 miles west on Interstate 70 to the Loma exit. Turn left and travel over the interstate, then turn right onto the frontage road and go 0.1 mile to a dirt road on the left. Turn left over a cattle guard and follow the road for 1.2 miles to a large parking area on the right with a BLM kiosk, day pavillion, and picnic tables.

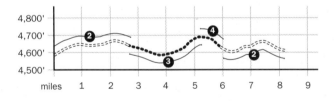

The Ride

0.0 From the parking area, go right on the doubletrack road, following the signs for Mary's Loop for 2 miles.

2.0 Go left up the short, steep hill to a gate and cattle guard.

2.2 Go through the gate and drop down a steep hill to a trail junction on the left.

2.6 Lion's Loop goes up and right; the Lower Lion's Loop Trail makes a sharp left onto a tight single-track trail that parallels the road. Follow the single-track down to a road.

2.7 Cross the road and drop down rocky tread into a dry wash (3+) onto the Lower Lion's Loop Trail.

3.3 Great views out to the Colorado River. Use caution, as the trail runs parallel to the side of a cliff with steep drop-offs.

4.0 Pedal through a short technical section (5) or, better yet, just carry your bike through this section.

4.5 Bear right on singletrack and begin a steep (4+) climb away from the river. The grade eases; cruise down to a trail junction.

5.2 Spur road; continue straight to a trail junction.

5.8 Go left on tight singletrack back up to the Lion's Loop Trailhead.

6.0 Retrace your route to the parking area.

8.6 Arrive back at your car.

Troy Built Trail
See map on page 58.

Location: 10 miles west of Fruita.

Distance: 7.8-mile loop.

Time: 1.5 to 2.5 hours.

Tread: 3.9 miles on singletrack; 3.9 miles on doubletrack.

Aerobic level: Moderate with some steep hills.

Technical difficulty: 4+ on the uphill singletrack; 3 on the doubletrack.

Hazards: Some very rocky sections on tight singletrack. Watch out for other cyclists and trail users.

Highlights: One of the finest rides in the area. The single-track riding is just awesome. The views to the Colorado River are beautiful, and the surrounding desert makes this a unique mountain bike ride.

Land status: BLM.

Maps: USGS Mesa County.

Access: From Fruita, travel 10 miles west on Interstate 70 to the Mack exit. Turn left, going under the interstate to a parking area on the frontage road. The ride starts here.

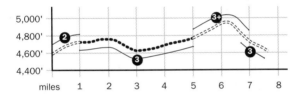

The Ride

0.0 From the parking area, go west (right) on the frontage road to the start of the Troy Built Trail.

1.1 Pass a BLM kiosk and begin a short, steep climb on excellent singletrack. Grind through a short, rocky section (3+) and follow the tight singletrack to a trail junction. This section of the trail is very tight singletrack. Use caution here and yield to other cyclists.

2.4 The Kokopelli Trail goes down and right; go up and left on tight singletrack. Singletrack riding does not get much better than this. Follow the trail through several washes and crank up a steep, loose, rocky hill (4) to a junction with the Lion's Loop Trail.

5.0 Go left up the wide, rocky doubletrack Lion's Loop Trail.

6.0 Stay right and begin a fast downhill to the frontage road.

6.2 Bear right.

6.6 Use caution as you fly down this very steep, rocky downhill.

6.9 Go right on the frontage road up to the parking area.

7.8 Arrive back at your car.

The Grand Loop

Location: 6 miles west of Fruita.

Distance: 22.2-mile loop.

Time: 2.5 hours to 4 hours.

Tread: 8 miles on doubletrack; 14.2 miles on singletrack.

•The Grand Loop

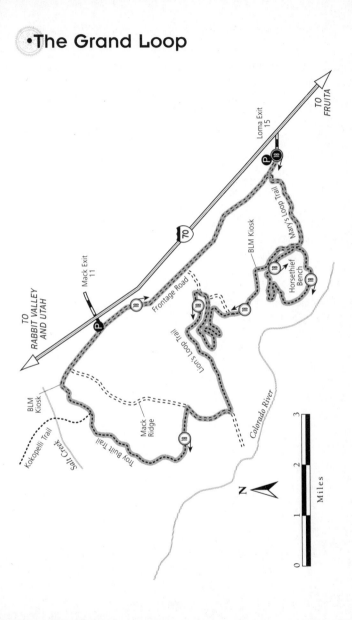

TO FRUITA

Loma Exit 15

Mary's Loop Trail

BLM Kiosk

Horsethief Bench

70

Mack Exit 11

Frontage Road

Lion's Loop Trail

TO RABBIT VALLEY AND UTAH

BLM Kiosk

Kokopelli Trail

Salt Creek

Troy Built Trail

Mack Ridge

Colorado River

N

Miles

0 1 2 3

Aerobic level: Strenuous with a lot of hills. This is for expert cyclists only. Bring lots of water and energy food.

Technical difficulty: 4 to 5 on the singletrack sections; 3 on the doubletrack.

Hazards: This is a long ride on varying terrain. Expect some difficult riding on rocky, steep tread; steep drop-offs; and other trail users. Bring a lot of fluids and energy bars—you're going to need them.

Highlights: A great ride that covers a lot of ground on and around the Kokopelli Trail. Spectacular overlooks to the Colorado River, great singletrack riding, and some very technical tread are just a few of the highlights on this expert-level ride.

Land status: BLM.

Maps: USGS Mesa County.

Access: From Fruita, drive 5 miles west on Interstate 70 to the Loma exit. Turn left and travel over the interstate, then turn right onto the frontage road and go 0.1 mile to dirt road on the left. Turn left over a cattle guard and follow the road for 1.2 miles to a large parking area on the right.

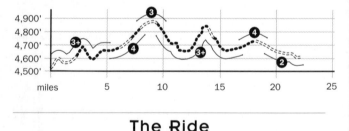

The Ride

0.0 From the parking area, go right on the dirt road, then make a quick left up the short hill following the well-marked Mary's Loop.

0.6 Go right up the rocky doubletrack trail. Cruise on excellent tread with beautiful views out to the Colorado River on the left.

1.9 Overlook to the Colorado River on the left.

2.1 Mary's Loop continues straight; you go left past the fence and drop down (4+) steep tread to the start of Horsethief Bench Loop.

2.2 Go left on awesome, tight singletrack that hugs the base of a cliff.

2.4 Great views of the Colorado River.

2.9 The trail drops down a short, steep wash, then parallels the Colorado River with steep drop-offs to the left.

3.8 The trail goes right, away from the river. A short hike-a-bike section leads to great singletrack riding.

4.9 The trail follows a dry streambed and then curves around the base of a sandstone wall on tight singletrack to complete the loop.

6.0 Crank left up the short, steep hill back to the Mary's Loop Trail.

6.1 Turn left onto Mary's Loop, then continue straight to the BLM kiosk and the start of the singletrack riding.

7.3 Continue straight on tight singletrack riding. Use caution: The trail hugs the edge of a large cliff with steep drop-offs.

7.7 Pass through a gate and crank up a short, steep hill. The tread becomes tight, rocky, and (3+) technical.

8.6 Trail junction. Go left on the new Steve's Cutoff connector trail. Tight singletrack riding leads down to a trail junction.

9.1 Go left. Watch out for steep drop-offs as you cruise along this beautiful trail with great views out to the Colorado River.

9.7 Pedal through a short technical section (5) or, better yet, just carry your bike through this section.

10.2 Bear right on singletrack and begin a steep (4+) climb away from the river. The grade eases; cruise down to a trail junction.

10.9 Spur road; continue straight to a trail junction.

11.5 Go left on tight singletrack back up to the Lion's Loop Trailhead.

11.6 Turn left onto the well-marked Lion's Loop Trail. Climb up past a register on rocky tread to level ground.

12.2 The tread becomes rocky and the view out to the Colorado River becomes even more impressive.

13.5 The trail takes a sharp right up through a very rocky section. Climb off your bike and carry it through this section. The trail stays very rocky and wanders down to a junction with a dirt road.

13.9 Go right up the rocky, loose road climbing up to a junction with the Troy Built Trail.

14.7 Junction with the Troy Built Trail. Turn left onto the Troy Built Trail. Drop down a steep hill on tight, rocky singletrack. Follow the obvious singletrack trail to a junction with the Kokopelli Trail.

17.3 The Kokopelli Trail goes left down to Salt Creek. You continue straight on the Troy Built Trail through a dry wash and up a steep hill (3+) to level ground.

18.6 The singletrack ends at a BLM kiosk. Follow the obvious doubletrack road back to the parking area.

22.2 Arrive back at your car.

Rabbit Valley Area

Kokopelli Trail/ Troy Built Trail

Location: 15 miles west of Fruita.

Distance: 17.5 miles one-way.

Time: 2.5 to 3.5 hours.

Tread: 8.5 miles on singletrack; 9 miles on doubletrack.

Aerobic level: Strenuous. This is a fairly long ride on excellent tread. Bring lots of water.

Technical difficulty: 4 on the singletrack descent to Salt Creek; 2 to 3 on the doubletrack.

Hazards: Steep, rocky descent to and climb up from Salt Creek. Watch out for traffic on the dirt road.

Highlights: Great views out to the Book Cliffs and down to the Colorado River. The singletrack section is steep and technical. This is great riding for advanced cyclists. The ride uses sections of three different trails to create a wonderful mountain bike experience. This ride can be done out and back, but I recommend doing a shuttle. Leave a car at the large parking area on the frontage road at the Mack exit just off Interstate 70.

•Kokopelli Trail/Troy Built Trail

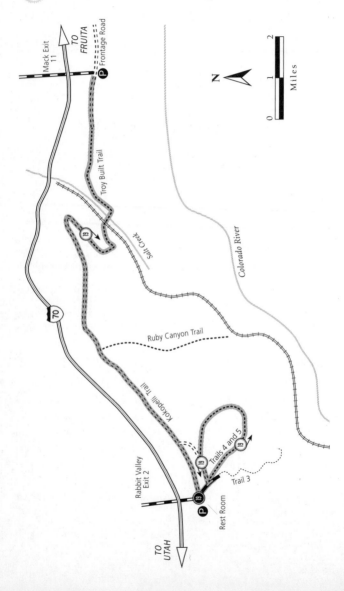

Land status: BLM.

Maps: USGS Mesa County.

Access: From Fruita, travel west on Interstate 70 for 15 miles to the Rabbit Valley exit. Go left over the highway to the first road on the left (Kokopelli Trail), turn left, and park in a large parking area with rest rooms on the left.

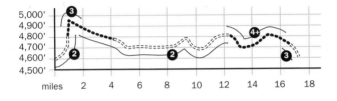

The Ride

0.0 From the parking area, turn left onto the Kokopelli Trail.

0.1 Turn right just past the cattle guard, following the sign for Trails 3, 4, and 5.

0.2 The trail forks; go left following the signs for Trails 4 and 5.

0.4 Trail 4 forks; take the right singletrack fork into open rangeland.

1.2 Begin an extended climb on tight singletrack. Crank through several short, steep (4) sections up to the ridge.

1.9 The trail drops down a steep hill to a trail junction.

2.1 Go left, following Trail 4.

2.3 Turn left onto tight, beautiful singletrack, still following Trail 4.

3.0 Junction with Trail 5; go left.

3.6 Junction with Trail 4; continue straight.

3.7	Cross over a road to singletrack. Continue straight to a trail junction.
4.2	Go left on a dirt road.
4.5	Go right on a dirt road.
4.6	Turn right and head back to the parking area.
4.9	Go right on the wide Kokopelli Trail.
6.6	Trail junction just past a corral. Continue straight.
7.1	Trail junction; continue straight.
7.8	The trail runs parallel to Interstate 70.
8.3	Great views out to the Book Cliffs.
8.9	Crank up a short hill and over a cattle guard. Continue straight past Ruby Canyon on the right. Drop down a steep hill to a trail junction.
10.0	Go right onto a wide dirt road.
10.1	The trail forks; go left. Follow the road down into a nice canyon. Then make the gradual uphill climb to Salt Creek Overlook.
12.2	Continue straight to a trail junction.
12.5	Go right on the singletrack Kokopelli Trail.
12.6	BLM register. Stop here for great views to Ruby Canyon and the Colorado River. The next mile is tight, rocky downhill (4) singletrack to Salt Creek. Use caution here.
13.5	Dismount and walk this short section. Follow the tight singletrack up past several short, technical (4) sections. Drop down to Salt Creek and under the railroad track to a bridge.
14.7	Cross the bridge and walk or ride up a steep hill to a trail junction.
14.9	The Kokopelli Trail goes right; you go left on the Troy Built Trail. Pedal through a dry wash; crank up a long hill on tight singletrack to level ground. Contour along the side of the hill, then drop down into a short slickrock section. Crank up a short hill to a dirt road.

16.4 Continue straight to a parking area on the right.

17.5 Arrive at your shuttle.

Rabbit Valley Trails 4 and 5

Location: 15 miles west of Fruita.

Distance: 5-mile loop.

Time: 30 minutes to 1 hour.

Tread: 3 miles on singletrack; 2 miles on doubletrack.

Aerobic level: Easy with a couple of short, steep, rocky hills.

Technical difficulty: Most of the riding is level 2, with a couple of short technical sections that can easily be walked.

Hazards: Short, steep, rocky sections and a tight single-track descent. This popular multiuse area sees a lot of traffic from ATV users.

Highlights: Great singletrack riding in the open desert—the scenic beauty is worth the trip itself. Throw in a great beginner ride and Rabbit Valley Dinosaur Site just across the highway and you have a ride that should be done by all cyclists passing through the area.

Land status: BLM.

Maps: USGS Mesa County.

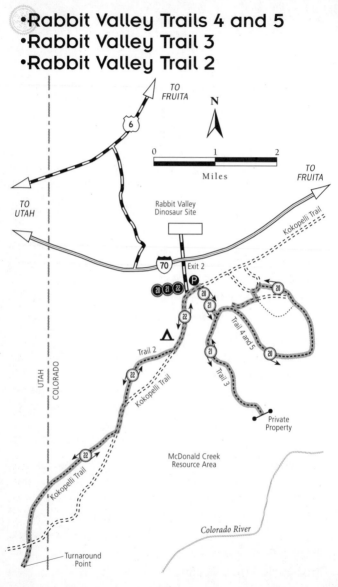

•Rabbit Valley Trails 4 and 5
•Rabbit Valley Trail 3
•Rabbit Valley Trail 2

TO
FRUITA

N

TO
FRUITA

TO
UTAH

Rabbit Valley
Dinosaur Site

Kokopelli Trail

Exit 2

P

Trail 4 and 5

Trail 2

Kokopelli Trail

Trail 3

Private
Property

McDonald Creek
Resource Area

UTAH
COLORADO

Kokopelli Trail

Colorado River

Turnaround
Point

0   1   2
Miles

Access: From Fruita, travel west on Interstate 70 for 15 miles to the Rabbit Valley exit. Go left over the highway to the first road on the left (Kokopelli Trail), turn left, and park in a large parking area with rest rooms on the left.

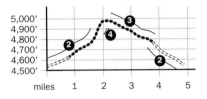

The Ride

0.0 From the parking area, turn left onto the Kokopelli Trail.

0.1 Turn right just past the cattle guard following the sign for Trails 3, 4, and 5.

0.2 The trail forks; go left, following the signs for Trails 4 and 5.

0.4 Trail 4 forks; take the right singletrack fork into open rangeland.

1.2 Begin an extended climb on tight singletrack. Crank through several short, steep (4) sections up to the ridge.

1.9 The trail drops down a steep hill to a trail junction.

2.1 Go left, following Trail 4.

2.3 Turn left onto tight, beautiful singletrack, still following Trail 4.

3.0 Junction with Trail 5; go left.

3.6 Junction with Trail 4; continue straight.

3.7 Cross over a road to singletrack. Continue straight to a trail junction.

4.2	Go left onto a dirt road.
4.5	Go right onto a dirt road.
4.6	Turn right onto the same doubletrack you rode in on and head back to the parking area.
5.0	Arrive back at your car.

Rabbit Valley Trail 3

See map on page 74.

Location: 15 miles west of Fruita.

Distance: 4.7 miles out and back.

Time: 30 minutes to 1 hour.

Tread: 3.9 miles on singletrack; 0.8 mile on doubletrack.

Aerobic level: Easy with a few short, steep hills.

Technical difficulty: 2 to 3 on singletrack; 1 on double-track.

Hazards: Beginners will walk a couple of steep hills. Watch out for ATV users and horse traffic. This popular multiuse area sees a lot of traffic.

Highlights: A great beginner singletrack, this excellent short ride will put a smile on most riders' faces. The Rabbit Valley Dinosaur Site is just across the interstate and well worth the time to visit.

Land Status: BLM.

Maps: USGS Mesa County.

Access: From Fruita, travel west on Interstate 70 for 15 miles to the Rabbit Valley exit. Go left over the highway to the first road on the left (Kokopelli Trail), turn left, and park in a large parking area with rest rooms on the left.

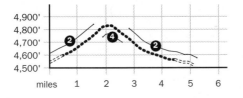

The Ride

0.0 From the parking area, go left on the Kokopelli Trail to a fence line at a cattle guard.

0.1 Turn right following the BLM signs for Trails 3, 4, and 5.

0.2 The trail forks; continue straight following the well-marked Trail 3.

0.4 The tread turns to singletrack and runs very close to a fence line before cutting across several dry washes up to a steep hill.

1.6 A short hike-a-bike section up a steep hill for most riders.

2.1 Another short, steep, rocky hill. Feel free to walk this section.

2.3 The ride ends here. The trail beyond is private property. Turn around and retrace your route to your car.

4.7 Arrive back at the parking area.

Rabbit Valley Trail 2

See map on page 74.

Location: 15 miles west of Fruita.

Distance: 11.2 miles out and back.

Time: 1.5 to 2 hours.

Tread: 10 miles on singletrack; 1.2 miles on doubletrack.

Aerobic level: Moderate with a few steep hills to keep you honest.

Technical difficulty: 4 on singletrack; 1 on doubletrack.

Hazards: Some steep, rocky sections and other trail users.

Highlights: A great, moderate singletrack ride that takes you out to a mesa overlooking the Colorado River. This is a remote ride in a beautiful desert environment.

Land status: BLM.

Maps: USGS Mesa County.

Access: From Fruita, travel west on Interstate 70 for 15 miles to the Rabbit Valley exit. Go left over the highway to the first road on the left (Kokopelli Trail), turn left, and park in a large parking area with rest rooms on the left.

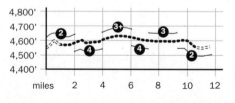

The Ride

0.0 From the parking area, follow the Kokopelli Trail for a short distance. Make a quick right onto the well-marked Trail 2. Ignore all side trails and stay on Trail 2 for the next 5 miles.

0.8 Follow the Kokopelli Trail for a short distance, making a quick right back onto Trail 2.

1.9 Cross over a road following Trail 2.

2.2 Follow the Kokopelli Trail straight for a short distance down past a camping area.

2.3 Continue straight to Trail 2.

2.5 Go right on Trail 2. Here the tread becomes tight singletrack and cuts a wonderful line through the desert.

3.4 Trail junction with a doubletrack road. Continue straight on tight singletrack up a steep, loose, rocky hill. Use caution (4) on the descent.

4.0 Begin a nice, long climb (3+) up to a flat area.

4.6 Take a break here and enjoy the beautiful desert.

5.0 Arrive at a junction with the Kokopelli Trail. Cross over the road to a sandy doubletrack trail. Follow the trail to where it ends at an overlook.

5.6 The road ends here. Take a break and enjoy the views down to the Colorado River. Turn around and pedal back to the Kokopelli Trail.

6.2 Cross the road and follow Trail 2 back to the parking area.

11.2 Arrive back at your car.

Kokopelli

The Kokopelli Trail is a 142-mile-long trail that extends from Loma, Colorado, in the east to Moab, Utah, in the west. The route follows a series of well-marked trails, doubletrack, and four-wheel-drive roads through some of the most breathtaking, astonishing scenery of the Colorado Plateau. Sections of the Kokopelli Trail follow closely along the beautiful Colorado River. As in the legend of Kokopelli the fertility god, the water of the Colorado River brings life to this area of the desert Southwest. You can take a day to explore a section of the Kokopelli Trail or take a week to experience the entire route. There are several convenient places to camp, and most of the trail is on public land.

But Just Who Is Kokopelli?

He's the most recognizable figure of the Four Corners area of the western United States. More popular, in fact, than Edward Abbey, Wallace Stegner, Bruce Babbit, John Nichols, or even Tony Hillerman, Kokopelli is the universal figure of fertility and is found on pottery and in petroglyphs dating as far back as 3,000 years. This flute-playing, ancient Toltec trader traveled routes between Mexico and the western United States, carrying a bag of seeds, dentalium shells, and macaw feathers. His flute announced his arrival to the many villages where he traded his precious goods.

He was also quite a lover and is recognized by many Native Americans of the Southwest as the symbol of fertility. He brings life to everything on this earth, both plants and animals. Legend has it that to be chosen as his companion for "dreamtime" was one of the greatest honors; several women bore children from these beautiful unions.

The name *Kokopelli* is derived from the Hopi words *koko* for "wood" and *pilau* for "hump," the ever-present sack that Kokopelli used to carry seeds of fruits and vegetables that he scattered over the barren land. Kokopelli also used his flute to bring warmth and make seeds grow. So that figure you see on key chains, shirts, jewelry, artwork, and pottery is really a sacred image of love and fertility, for the earth and for all humanity.

So—if you're out on the Kokopelli Trail and you see a desert flower blooming and hear the soft, flutelike music of the wind, you'll know you have experienced the beauty of Kokopelli.

Appendix A

Resources

Bureau of Land Management
2815 H Road
Grand Junction, CO 81506
Phone 970–244–3000
Fax 970–244–3083

Colorado Division of Wildlife
6060 Broadway
Denver, CO 80216
Phone 303–297–1192

Colorado Plateau Mountain
Bike Trail Association
P.O. Box 4602
Grand Junction, CO 81502
Phone 970–243–0663
www.copmoba.com

Fruita Chamber of Commerce
325 East Aspen Avenue
Fruita, CO 81521
Phone 970–858–3894

Grand Valley Mountain Bike
Patrol
380 Ridgeway Drive
Grand Junction, CO 81503
Phone 970–245–0032
E-mail kfoote@gj.net

IMBA
P.O. Box 7578
Boulder, CO 80806
Phone 888–442–4622
www.imba.com

Appendix B

Bike Shops

The Board and Buckle Company
2822 North Avenue
Grand Junction, CO 81504
Phone 970–242–9285

Mountainside Bikes and Blades
2454 Highway 6 and 50
Grand Junction, CO 81504
Phone 970–241–4340

Over the Edge Sports
202 East Aspen Avenue
Fruita, CO 81512
Phone 800–873–3068
E-mail edge@gj.net
www.gj.net/~edge

Thompkins Cycle Sports
301 Main
Grand Junction, CO 81502
Phone 970–241–0141

Appendix C

Events

Fruita Fat-Tire Festival, 202 East Aspen Avenue, Fruita, Colorado 81521; 800–873–3068. A great mountain bike celebration held every year during the last weekend of April. This is a fun weekend packed with mountain bike activities that attract cyclists from all over the world. Come join the fun at one of the premier mountain bike events in the nation.

Ches-Peach Ride, Race, and Roast, 202 East Aspen Avenue, Fruita, Colorado 81521; 800–873–3068. A mountain bike celebration held every year during the middle of October. Pack up the bikes and enjoy some great riding, racing, and food in one of America's great mountain biking areas.

A Short Index of Rides

Sweet Singletrack
1 Roller Coaster
2 The Gunny Loop
3 Andy's Loop
5 Mira Monte/Lower Gunny Loop
6 Turkey Flats Loop
7 Prime Cut/Joe's Cutoff
8 Chutes and Ladders
9 Zippety Doo Daa
12 The Edge
14 Horsethief Bench
17 Troy Built Trail
18 The Grand Loop
22 Rabbit Valley Trail 2

Technical Test
2 The Gunny Loop
4 The Ribbon
5 Mira Monte/Lower Gunny Loop
8 Chutes and Ladders
9 Zippety Doo Daa
11 The Frontside
12 The Edge
17 Troy Built Trail
18 The Grand Loop
19 Kokopelli Trail/Troy Built Trail

Beginner's Luck
7 Prime Cut
10 Vegetarian Loop
13 Mary's Loop
20 Rabbit Valley Trails 4 and 5
21 Rabbit Valley Trail 3

Great Climbs
2 The Gunny Loop
4 The Ribbon
6 Turkey Flats Loop
9 Zippety Doo Daa
11 The Frontside
12 The Edge
15 Lion's Loop
18 The Grand Loop

Great Downhills
1 Roller Coaster
2 The Gunny Loop
4 The Ribbon
8 Chutes and Ladders
9 Zippety Doo Daa
11 The Frontside
12 The Edge
15 Lion's Loop
17 Troy Built Trail
18 The Grand Loop

Glossary

ATB: All-terrain bicycle; aka mountain bike, sprocket rocket, fat-tire flier.

ATV: All-terrain vehicle; in this book *ATV* refers to motorbikes and three- and four-wheelers designed for off-road use.

Bail: Getting off the bike, usually in a hurry, and whether or not you mean to. Often a last resort.

Bunny hop: Leaping up, while riding, and lifting both wheels off the ground to jump over an obstacle (or for sheer joy).

Clamper cramps: That burning, cramping sensation experienced in the hands during extended braking.

Clean: To ride without touching a foot (or other body part) to the ground; to ride a tough section successfully.

Clipless: A type of pedal with a binding that accepts a special cleat on the soles of bike shoes. The cleat clicks in for more control and efficient pedaling and out for safe landings (in theory).

Contour: A line on a topographic map showing a continuous elevation level over uneven ground. Also used as a verb to indicate a fairly easy or moderate grade: "The trail contours around the canyon rim before the final grunt to the top."

Dab: To put a foot or hand down (or hold on to or lean on a tree or other support) while riding. If you have to dab, then you haven't ridden that piece of trail **clean**.

Downfall: Trees that have fallen across the trail.

Doubletrack: A trail, jeep road, ATV route, or other track with two distinct ribbons of **tread**, typically with grass growing in between. No matter which side you choose, the other rut always looks smoother.

Endo: Lifting the rear wheel off the ground and riding (or abruptly not riding) on the front wheel only. Also known, at various degrees of control and finality, as a nose wheelie, "going over the handlebars," and a face plant.

Fall line: The angle and direction of a slope; the **line** you follow when gravity is in control and you aren't.

Graded: When a gravel road is scraped level to smooth out the washboards and potholes, it has been graded. In this book, a road is described as graded only if it is regularly maintained. Not all such roads are graded every year, however.

Granny gear: The lowest (easiest) gear, a combination of the smallest of the three chainrings on the bottom bracket spindle (where the pedals and crank arms attach to the bike's frame) and the largest cog on the rear cluster. Shift down to your granny gear for serious climbing.

Hammer: To ride hard; derived from how it feels afterward: "I'm hammered."

Hammerhead: Someone who actually enjoys feeling **hammered**. A Type-A-personality rider who goes hard and fast all the time.

Kelly hump: An abrupt mound of dirt across the road or trail. These are common on old logging roads and skidder tracks, placed there to block vehicle access. At high speeds, they become launching pads for bikes and inadvertent astronauts.

Line: The route (or trajectory) between or over obstacles or through turns. **Tread** or trail refers to the ground you're riding on; the line is the path you choose within the tread (and exists mostly in the eye of the beholder).

Off-the-seat: Moving your butt behind the bike seat and over the rear tire; used for control on extremely steep descents. This position increases braking power, helps prevent **endos**, and reduces skidding.

Portage: To carry the bike, usually up a steep hill, across unridable obstacles, or through a stream.

Quads: Thigh muscles (short for quadriceps)—or maps in the USGS topographic series (short for quadrangles). Nice quads of either kind can help get you out of trouble in the backcountry.

Ratcheting: Also known as backpedaling; pedaling backward to avoid hitting rocks or other obstacles with the pedals.

Sidehill: Where the trail crosses a slope. If the **tread** is narrow, keep your inside (uphill) pedal up to avoid hitting the ground. If the tread tilts downhill, you may have to use some body language to keep the bike plumb or vertical to avoid slipping out.

Singletrack: A trail, game run, or other track with only one ribbon of **tread**. Good singletrack is pure fun.

Spur: A side road or trail that splits off from the main route.

Surf: Riding through loose gravel or sand, when the wheels sway from side to side. Also heavy surf: frequent and difficult obstacles.

Suspension: A bike with front suspension has a shock-absorbing fork or stem. Rear suspension absorbs shock between the rear wheel and frame. A bike with both is said to be fully suspended.

Switchbacks: When a trail goes up a steep slope, it zigzags or switchbacks across the **fall line** to ease the gradient of the climb. Well-designed switchbacks make a turn with at least an 8-foot radius and remain fairly level within the turn itself. These are rare, however, and cyclists often struggle to ride through sharply angled, sloping switchbacks.

Track stand: Balancing on a bike in one place, without rolling forward appreciably. Cock the front wheel to one side and bring that pedal up to the one or two o'clock position. Now control your side-to-side balance by applying pressure on the pedals and brakes and changing the angle of the front wheel, as needed. It takes practice but really comes in handy at stoplights, on **switchbacks**, and when trying to free a foot before falling.

Tread: The riding surface, particularly regarding **singletrack**.

Water bar: A log, rock, or other barrier placed in the **tread** to divert water off the trail and prevent erosion. Peeled logs can be slippery and cause bad falls, especially when they angle sharply across the trail.

Whoop-dee-doo: A series of **kelly humps** used to keep vehicles off trails. Watch your speed or do the dreaded top tube tango.